Mantras from a Poet: Jessica Powers

Robert F. Morneau

Illustrations by
Sr. Doris Klein, CSA

Sheed & Ward

The author acknowledges the generous and expert assistance of these people who contributed their time and talent to make this book possible:

Sr. Doris Klein, CSA for the illustrations;
Sr. Miriam Cecile Ross, S.S.N.D. for the music;
Sister Mary de Sales Hoffmann, O.S.F. and Sister Marie Isabel McElrone, O.S.F. for editorial assistance.

Sheed & Ward™ is a service of National Catholic Reporter Publishing Company, Inc.

Library of Congress Cataloging-in-Publication Data

Morneau, Robert F.
    Mantras from a poet : Jessica Powers / Robert F. Morneau.
        p. cm.
    ISBN: 1-55612-420-1 (pbk.)
    1. Meditations. 2. Prayers. 3. Christian poetry, American.
I. Powers, Jessica. II. Title.
    BX2182.2.M6685   1991   90-64032
    242—dc20   CIP

Published by: Sheed & Ward
                115 E. Armour Blvd. P.O. Box 419492
                Kansas City, MO 64141
To order, call: (800) 333-7373

Contents

Acknowledgments

Letters of Rainer Maria Rilke: 1892-1910. Translated by Jane Bannard Greene and M.D. Herter Norton. New York: W.W. Norton and Company, 1945.

The New American Bible, copyright© 1970 by the Confraternity of Christian Doctrine, Washington, D.C., used by permission of said copyright owner. No part of *The New American Bible* may be reproduced in any form without permission in writing from the Confraternity of Christian Doctrine, Washington, D.C.

The Lion, The Witch, and the Wardrobe. C.S. Lewis.

John Cassian: Conferences, trans. and preface by Colm Luebheid with introduction by Owen Chadwick (New York: Paulist Press, 1985).

Johannes Baptist Metz, *Poverty of Spirit,* translated by John Drury (New York: Paulist Press, 1968).

The Hidden Ground of Love by Thomas Merton.

Douglas Steere, *On Beginning from Within—On Listening to Another* (New York: Harper & Row, Publishers, 1943).

Bernard of Clairvaux: Selected Works, translation and foreword by G.R. Evans, introduction by Jean Leclercq, O.S.B., preface by Ewert H. Cousins (New York: Paulist Press, 1987).

The Creative Work: Canon as a Model for Biblical Education by Walter Brueggemann, copyright© 1982 Fortress Press. Used by permission of Augsburg Fortress.

The Sacrament of the Present Moment by Jean-Pierre de Caussade, translated by Kitty Muggeridge. Copyright English translation ©1981 by William Collins Sons and Company, Inc. Reprinted by permission of HarperCollins Publishers.

Madeleine L'Engle, *Walking on Water: Reflections on Faith and Art* (Wheaton, IL: Harold Shaw Publishers, © Crosswicks, 1980).

Preface

On August 18, 1988, Jessica Powers died at the age of 83. In 1941, she entered the Carmel of the Mother of God in Milwaukee, Wisconsin, and spent the rest of her life as a Carmelite nun taking the religious name Sister Miriam of the Holy Spirit.

I had the great privilege of meeting Jessica Powers in the autumn of 1985. Over the next three years I discovered that she had written over four hundred poems, almost three hundred of which were published; I found her to be a listener and lover, following Christ in the Carmelite tradition. A warm, witty, gracious human being she loved life and embraced the sufferings and joys that God sent to her. Our correspondence from 1985 to 1988 was quite limited, approximately thirty cards and brief letters. Several of her personal notes give us a glimpse of her spirituality and values. Here are a few excerpts from the letters.

July 15, 1985

I still miss our old monastic custom of reading at meals; one had all this spiritual input, which could be neglected if left to another busier time of day. But I realize that most Sisters prefer talking at meals. . . Enclosed are two poems which you may like; the one by e. e. cummings is a recent finding; isn't it lovely? "To merciful Him whose only now is forever . . ." And the one by Mark Van Doren reminds me of what Our Father St. John of the Cross said of the glance of God: how when God looks at a soul He makes it beautiful.

Thanksgiving Day, '85

First of all, thank you for your nice visit, which was enjoyable and a grace; it was good of you to come so far out of your way. I was happy to meet you, knowing you from your writings. You have lots of riches to share, and I was sorry afterward that I was so talkative.". . . "In your letter you suggested—commanded!—that I give more time to writing. At the moment I can't, for obvious reasons—we are busier than bees. But I do try to write a little now and then. *The Bible Today* just took two poems, but of course it will probably be months before they are printed. One, "The Leftovers," was inspired by a homily that Bishop Sklba gave when he came to say Mass for us (the gospel was on the multiplication of the loaves). He spoke of "leftovers."

January 23, 1986

Now that it is Ordinary Time again, and there is a bit of a lull, I have been reading your *Mantras for the Midnight* and finding many rich and lovely things. Of your Mantra books, I think this is my favorite (though all are inspiring). We need that dimension of sadness in our lives, don't we? It seems as if the best literature and art has that undercurrent of sorrow. Don't you think, too, that when we are alone in a quiet place we have a clearer vision, a deeper awareness? This seems true especially when we are away from familiar places and people. When I was in New York, I recall, I could hardly bear the beautiful music that drifted up to me from a lower apartment. The sadness wasn't a loneliness for people; I'm not sure it was even loneliness. Just too much beauty for the human heart to bear. That is why, I think, that solitude-and-silence is prescribed for our life (and in a measure for every life) because one seldom has deep thoughts and feelings amid distraction and noise.

Your quotations were very well chosen; there were many choice ones I had never seen. And I liked your personal comments and explanations of the mantras. The pictures, too, were very apropos. That picture of the railroad was very effective; I can hear our Mother Paula of happy memory saying that when the train whistles and goes off in the distance it seems to be saying, "I am going away . . . away . . ." And as Lacordaire said, every parting is surely a taste of death. Other pictures too: the seashore, abandoned buildings, wreckage, lonely

places—all added to the mood of the book. And of course lonely people, and the tragedy of so many suffering or wasted lives. I think of
what Edna St. Vincent Millay wrote:

> The anguish of the world is on my tongue; It sickens me; it is
> more than I can eat. Blessed are the toothless old and the tooth-
> less young Who cannot rend the meat.

April 7, 1986

For an Order like ours, dedicated to silence and solitude as a back-
ground for prayer, it was a reproach that we do not get more extended
silences into our lives. I had known little about the Quakers.

May 29, 1986

Some poems were inspired by what I read or heard, but "The Garments of God" was written out of my own heart—my experience of
God when I did not think I was pleasing to Him.

I enjoyed the excerpt from Herbert—yes, it surely is a time to "relish versing." I never remember a lovelier springtime, even though it
was chilly—and dismal!—at times, too. The lilacs and snowball and
flowering trees, etc., outdid themselves in beauty. Even when it
rained—it was refreshing to have all that "wet and wildness." We
thought this winter was especially scenic and beautiful, in spite of the
fact that it began so early and lasted so long that it wore out its welcome.

October 31, 1986

We loved your little angels; they are a precious treasure. We opened
the box at recreation, and all the Sisters exclaimed over the delightful
surprise. They were exquisitely done. May God bless and reward you!
There was something remarkable, too, in their arrival at this time. We
had been having video-tapes the last three weeks—every Wednesday—
and of course we have been talking and thinking about the angels a

great deal, and making resolves to pray to our angels more, and to the angels of others to whom we wish to do good. And to the angels around the tabernacle. And to the angels around us when we receive the Holy Eucharist. I think of a holy card that my aunt (who was a Sister of Mercy) gave me when I was a little girl—her jubilee card, with a beautiful angel on it and the words: "O sublime vow of obedience! How sweet are thy bonds to a soul that gives itself generously to God!" I was fascinated with the angel. I brought the card to Carmel, but it got lost when someone borrowed my breviary. I still hope to find it in a book somewhere. How about that for detachment? Anyway, I think that card influenced my life: a small hint of the beauty of holiness. We never know when or where a seed that is planted grows, do we? Some little thing can be a source of grace.

Ash Wednesday, 1987

I am glad that you introduced me to the Shakers. I like their thoughts on "harvesting," as I was inspired by their thoughts on silence, which you sent me. There are graces in writings of those not of our faith, aren't there? Sometimes lovely things that are lost. Beautiful things God scatters everywhere. As Walt Whitman said, (in other words), that God is tossing down love letters in the streets and everywhere, if only we would watch out for them. I think I have come to see that even the contradictions and crosses of life are His "love letters." I've begun to look for them with a certain joy—signs that tell me that Jesus is near. The unexpected delay, the negative response, the inopportune caller, the gimmick that won't work, the nice food that got overcooked, the lack of something needed, the ballpoint pen that smudges, the mistake one can't undo—the list is endless! Not (I hope) that I concentrate on the unpleasant things but that they are little signs that I share in the life of Jesus. They are so much richer than the penances I pick out for myself.

* * *

Preface   ix

In the summer of 1989, Sheed and Ward (Kansas City) published
Selected Poetry of Jessica Powers, a manuscript that Jessica Powers
herself approved, making the final selections of what was to be in-
cluded and what was not. Within five months, the book was into its
second printing. In August of 1989 a symposium on the life and work
of Jessica Powers was held at Marquette University. Two hundred and
eighty people attended the day of lectures and sharing. The five manu-
scripts from that symposium were printed under the guidance of Fr.
Bernard O. McGarty (*Times Review*, Box 4004, La Crosse, WI., 54602-
4004). The quarterly magazine *Spiritual Life* also published three of the
lectures. Perhaps Jessica Powers may one day be recognized as a sig-
nificant American religious poet. Her verse has clarity, depth and an
evocative power that few religious poets can match. When I first read
the privately published collection *The House of Rest*, I hoped to find at
least a few poems that would move me. Unexpectedly, one poem after
another spoke deeply to me of our common faith journey. These poems
continue to inspire and challenge my faith.

This present volume of mantras, fifteen in number, is a gesture of a
gift to someone I am eternally indebted to. May *Mantras from a Poet*
provide a beginning of a life-long friendship with a dedicated religious,
a talented poet and a wonderful, warm and loving human being.

Springtime

MANTRA: **Hurry me into springtime**

SOURCE: Jessica Powers' "Come, South Wind"

"By south wind is meant the Holy Spirit who awakens love."
                                            St. John of the Cross

Over and over I say to the south wind: come,
waken in me and warm me!
I have walked too long with a death's chill in the air,
mourned over trees too long with branches bare.
Ice has a falsity for all its brightness
and so has need of your warm reprimand.
A curse be on the snow that lapsed from whiteness,
and all bleak days that paralyze my land.

I am saying all day to Love who wakens love:
rise in the south and come!
Hurry me into springtime; hustle the winter
out of my sight; make dumb
the north wind's loud impertinence. Then plunge me
into my leafing and my blossoming,
and give me pasture, sweet and sudden pasture.
Where could the Shepherd bring
his flocks to graze? Where could they rest at noonday?
O south wind, listen to the woe I sing!
One whom I love is asking for the summer
from me, who still am distances from spring.[1]
                                            (1954; 1984)

1

PARALLEL REFERENCES

My lover speaks; he says to me, "Arise, my beloved, my beautiful one, and come! The flowers appear on the earth, the time of pruning the vines has come, and the song of the dove is heard in our land. The fig tree puts forth its figs, and the vines, in bloom, give forth fragrance. Arise, my beloved, my beautiful one, and come!" (Song of Songs 2, 1-13)

* * *

Meanwhile, Mary stood weeping beside the tomb. Even as she wept, she stooped to peer inside, and there she saw two angels in dazzling robes. One was seated at the head and the other at the foot of the place where Jesus' body had lain. "Woman," they asked her, "why are you weeping?" She answered them, "Because the Lord has been taken away, and I do not know where they have put him." She had no sooner said this than she turned around and caught sight of Jesus standing there. (John 20, 11-14)

* * *

THE SOUTH WIND

"Hurry me into springtime," says the oak,

"Too long have I courted my sap,
Aching are my branches to break into flower,
Chilled my bark by the winter winds."

Hurry me into springtime,
Hurry me into springtime.

"Hurry me into springtime," says the groundhog,

"Too long has the sun abandoned my home,
too absent my shadow these February days,
too confining my damp dark burrow."

Hurry me into springtime,
Hurry me into springtime.

"Hurry me into springtime," says the sexton,

    "Too hard the burial ground,
    too sharp the spiral bells,
    too deep this human slumber."

                                       Hurry me into springtime,
                                       Hurry me into springtime.

PRAYER

    God of autumn and spring, God of winter and summer, give us the love that treasures all seasons. No matter where the sun or what the temperature, may your loving, warm presence give us life. Hurry all people into the springtime of your life. Amen.

                       * * *

QUOTATIONS FROM C. S. LEWIS[2]

    And in that silence Edmund could at last listen to the other noise properly. A strange, sweet, rustling, chattering noise—and yet not so strange, for he knew he'd heard it before—if only he could remember where! Then all at once he did remember. It was the noise of running water. All round them, though out of sight, bubbling, splashing and even (in the distance) roaring. And his heart gave a great leap (though he hardly knew why) when he realized that the frost was over. (114)

                       * * *

"This is no thaw," said the Dwarf, suddenly stopping. "This is *spring*. What are we to do? Your winter has been destroyed, I tell you! This is Aslan's doing." (118)

* * *

They [the Beaver and the children] had been just as surprised as Edmund when they saw the winter vanishing and the whole wood passing in a few hours or so from January to May. They hadn't even known for certain (as the Witch did) that this was what happened when Aslan came to Narnia. But they all knew that it was her spells which had produced the endless winter; and therefore they all knew when this magic spring began that something had gone wrong, and badly wrong, with the Witch's schemes. (120)

* * *

REFLECTION

Barren March branches hung but twelve yards from my childhood bedroom window. That opening to the world remained securely latched through spring storms and chilling March winds. With the disappearance of the snow and the rising of a more friendly sun, I knew that spring would come soon to our backyard once again. Gradually, the branches would become vibrant with life, the birds would return from the deep south, and a blanket of green would begin to spread over a naked world. I would soon gain a new freedom as my latched window would be thrown open in an act of magnanimous hospitality. My small heart could not absorb all that was to come.

A malady in those early years, and it has faithfully remained with me, was avarice. I longed to hold each month beyond its proper stay. March seduced me by her winds, April by her warm, soft showers. November spoke to the melancholy in my soul and July whispered her song of bold warmth. But during the winter months something would creep into my heart and whisper—hurry me into springtime—and then, with deep longing, I searched for the south wind. Springtime does not come for all people. The chronically depressed, the abused child, the lonely and afflicted can be held captive by their pain. Their latched, windowed hearts failed to find freedom. The knowledge that some are deprived tempers overjoy or overdesire. Not until we pray that communal prayer "hurry *us* into springtime" will full life touch our spirits. Springtime, like grace, is intended for all.

Even springtime has its melancholy. It is but a forerunner of summer and will not perdure. It serves as an instrument and agent for larger life. Such a humble role gives the spring a special nobility and beauty. Its willingness to die to give birth endears it to our hearts all the more.

Hurry me into springtime

COMMENTARY

THE SOUTH WIND

Lord God, there is something about repetition that disposes the human heart. "Over and over" we plead for your coming. That constant refrain breaks up our hardened soil and disposes us to your presence. At your arrival our winter sleepiness and dormancy vanish, our coldness melts away. No one can comprehend the meaning of life without you. We are lost in the cosmos and taste the horrendous pain of loneliness. Our hearts are void of affection and our consciousness too inattentive to your presence. Come, Lord Jesus, come and bring us your life.

WINTER WONDERLAND?

From a distance, Lord, winter does not appear harsh. Yet appearance can and often does deceive. Up close we know this season for what it is: trees left naked in freezing temperature; frigid air telling of the stirrings of death; ice, beautiful but treacherous; snow, paralyzing limbs. Come, Lord, bring your warmth and presence to the winter of our hearts. Drive far away all that opposes life. Send your Spirit and we shall live.

LOVE! LOVE!

From dawn to dusk my plea remains the same, Lord: "rise in the South and come." You are Love. I call you by name. When you come, the small seed of love, too deeply buried in my soul, will break forth and blossom. That seed will no longer be held captive by the winter's chill. Your Love comes to still my song of sadness. Your Love comes because your compassion is so great.

REQUEST

Lord, someone has asked life from me. Someone has requested a grazing ground, a haven of rest, the hospitality of my love. I have nothing of my own to bestow and yet that request haunts my winter days. To be asked for summer when spring has not yet arrived is so painful. Lord, are you that Someone? Is your request for summer your concern for your people? Come, O south wind, that I may say yes and share my/your love with all.

Kingdom

MANTRA: **the unspeakable wisdom**

SOURCE: Jessica Powers' "The Kingdom of God"

Not towards the stars, O beautiful naked runner,
not on the hills of the moon after a wild white deer,
seek not to discover afar the unspeakable wisdom,—
the quarry is here.

Beauty holds court within,—
a slim young virgin in a dim shadowy place.
Music is only the echo of her voice,
and earth is only a mirror for her face.

Not in the quiet arms, O sorrowful lover;
O fugitive, not in the dark on a pillow of breast;
hunt not under the lighted leaves for God,—
here is the sacred Guest.

There is a Tenant here.
Come home, roamer of earth, to this room and find
a timeless Heart under your own heart beating,
a Bird of beauty singing under your mind.[3]

* * *

PARALLEL REFERENCES

Now with you is Wisdom, who knows your works
    and was present when you made the world;
Who understands what is pleasing in your eyes
    and what is conformable with your commands.
Send her forth from your holy heavens

and from your glorious throne dispatch her
That she may be with me and work with me,
that I may know what is pleasing to you. (Wisdom 9, 9-10)

* * *

THE KINGDOM OF GOD
—the unspeakable wisdom
—the unspeakable wisdom

   —a quarry nearer than stars and moon

   —a queen of beauty reigning supreme

   —a quiver of harmony sung through the ages

—the unspeakable wisdom
—the unspeakable wisdom

   —a glimmer of light for all dark journeys

   —a glory mirrored in mountains and hills

   —a goal driving us home out of exile

—the unspeakable wisdom
—the unspeakable wisdom

   —a bird of beauty forever singing of love

   —a boarder who fails in joy in leave

   —a bride virginal in all purity

—the unspeakable wisdom
—the unspeakable wisdom

The un-speak-a-ble wis-dom — ; the un-speak-a-ble wis-dom.

PRAYER

Down too many days and nights we have chased after strange hopes and false dreams, O Lord. Beyond our own souls we have sought a counterfeit peace. Draw us back to you, gracious Beauty. May the beams of your wisdom, inexplicable and omnipotent, illumine the dark shadowy places of our hearts and our world. Then, gifted with an unspeakable wisdom of Jesus the Lord, we will experience your tender compassion, know for the first time the beauty of dawn, and be guided on the way of peace. May your kingdom come, your will be done.

QUOTATIONS FROM JOHN CASSIAN[4]

For those who travel without a marked road there is the toil of the journey—and no arrival at destination. (39)

* * *

For a mind which lacks an abiding sense of direction veers hither and yon by the hour, and by the minute is a prey to outside influences and is endlessly the prisoner of whatever strikes it first. (41)

* * *

Now there can be nothing else within us except the knowledge or unawareness of truth, the love of sin or of virtue, and with these we make a kingdom in the heart for the devil or for Christ. And what this kingdom is like is set out by the apostle when he says, "The kingdom of God does not consist of eating and drinking, but in righteousness and peace and joy in the holy spirit" (Rom 14, 17). If the kingdom of God is within us and that is a kingdom of justice, of peace, and of joy, then whoever remains with these virtues is certainly in the kingdom of God. By contrast, all who deal in unrighteousness, in discord, and in death-bearing gloom have taken their stand in the kingdom of the devil, in hell and in lifelessness. It is by these tokens that the kingdom of God or of the devil is recognized. (46-47)

* * *

REFLECTION

"A-ROVING"

As a young boy I was introduced to the sounds of the sea. It was in elementary school, while listening to the haunting melodies of sea chanteys, that my nomadic heart was swept away. Faraway places and distant ports called me forth. But then one day a chantey contained these lyrics: "I'll go no more a-roving from you, fair maid." There's something of the roamer in all of us. From Ponce de Leon, who sought the illusive fountain of youth, to modern explorers of space, we travel many miles in pursuit of wisdom and love, searching for some permanent residence for the affections of our hearts and the weariness of our bodies. Disconnected from the source of life by either ignorance or sin, we seek union and a modicum of peace. An alternative to roaming far from home is to make an inner journey, one that is more risky than space flights or the climbing of mountain peaks. Beneath our hearts and minds resides Wisdom. Our God dwells here as guest and tenant and we are challenged to find his lodging and to share a common life with our Creator. Just as astronauts need guidance in their spatial wanderings, so too all who make the journey within. St. Teresa of Avila describes the various rooms of the interior castle, the different types of presences and levels of prayer. She notes that the journey need not be made. Pilgrims can remain outside and never pass through the portal of prayer. But for those who dare to venture, what wonders and joys await them in their discovery of Wisdom. Our nomadic spirit can travel deep within. Is God enough for our insatiable appetites? Julian of Norwich answered yes: "God, of your goodness give me yourself, for you are enough for me, and I can ask for nothing which is less which can pay you full worship. And if I ask anything which is less, always I am in want; but only in you do I have everything." Some of us tend to go a-roving over and over again. Hopefully one day we will resist that temptation and be open to the grace to stay home and there to find Wisdom.

* * *

COMMENTARY

SEEK AND YOU SHALL FIND

Lord, each day, we your creatures seek to find someone or something that will fill the dark, lonely abyss within our hearts, that gnawing hunger in the pit of our stomachs, that unceasing thirst for intimacy. We seek afar the pearl of great price, as far as the distant stars of fame, reputation, success. We race to the moon in pursuit of undomesticated excellence, hoping that perhaps some extraordinary achievement will bring us peace. We are led astray in these wanderings, deceived by romanticized beauty. A lesson must be branded on our hearts: you are the quarry, you are the unspeakable wisdom, and you are HERE within our souls. As frantic runners we must stop the race, remove our shoes, embrace our nakedness and find within ourselves that beauty which is a faint reflection of the immortal Beauty that you are.

BEAUTY

Lord, St. Augustine once addressed you as beauty, "ever ancient, ever new." You are Wisdom, you are Beauty. Deep in the dark, dim, shadowy sanctuary of our souls you hold your court and counsel. Two clues are given us of the glory of your inner court: music and earth. Though only a faint echo of your voice, music suggests the profound unity and congruence of your inner life. Earth, in all its diverse riches, mirrors your splendor, however dimly. Lord, help us to make worthy that court within. Enable us to embrace the majesty of your wisdom and beauty.

SACRED GUEST

Stars and moon fail to fill the void in our lives. So we turn to those who are near, hoping that in the warm embrace of friends our sorrow might be turned into joy. Sad to say, the yearning of our hearts is not stilled. We flee then into the dark, longing for forbidden intimacy. Yet, even when we find it, our restlessness perdures and our sense of being eternal fugitives deepens. But the hunt and the race continues, Lord, in the world of nature, of possessions, of thrills. Again we find but a slight reflection of your wisdom and beauty. You have not housed yourself in any of these—you are guested here within our very hearts.

TENANT

A guest-turned-tenant are you, O Lord. You have come to stay; you are not passing through. You call us to stop our roaming and come home to our very selves. You are found within or nowhere. In the dim shadowy place of our souls your eternal heart beats. If only I could get past the ego of my own beating heart—if only I could experience that every heartbeat is a gift from you. And below my consciousness is the movement of your love and forgiveness and wisdom. In the beauty of the song we come to life, we enter your kingdom and your love.

* * *

Master Beggar

MANTRA: **I too would be a beggar**

SOURCE: Jessica Powers' "The Master Beggar"

Worse than the poorest mendicant alive,
the pencil man, the blind man with his breath
of music shaming all who do not give,
are You to me, Jesus of Nazareth.

Must You take up Your post on every block
of every street? Do I have no release?
Is there no room of earth that I can lock
to Your sad face, Your pitiful whisper "Please"?

I seek the counters of time's gleaming store
but make no purchases, for You are there.
How can I waste one coin while you implore
with tear-soiled cheeks and dark blood-matted hair?

And when I offer You in charity
pennies minted by love, still, still You stand
fixing Your sorrowful wide eyes on me.
Must all my purse be emptied in Your hand?

Jesus, my beggar, what would You have of me?
Father and mother? the lover I longed to know?
The child I would have cherished tenderly?
Even the blood that through my heart's valves flow?

I too would be a beggar. Long tormented,
I dream to grant You all and stand apart

With You on some bleak corner, tear-frequented,
and trouble mankind for its human heart.⁵

* * *

PARALLEL REFERENCES

The Lord God has given me a well-trained tongue,
That I might know how to speak to the weary
a word that will rouse them.
Morning after morning he opens my ear that I may hear;
And I have not rebelled, have not turned my back.
I gave my back to those who beat me,
my cheeks to those who plucked my beard;
My face I did not shield from buffets and spitting. (Is 50, 4-7)

* * *

As they led him away, they laid hold of one Simon the Cyrenean
who was coming in from the fields. They put a crossbeam on Simon's
shoulder for him to carry along behind Jesus. A crowd of people
followed him, including women who beat their breasts and lamented
over him. Jesus turned to them and said: "Daughters of Jerusalem, do
not weep for me. Weep for yourselves and for your children. The days
are coming when they will say, 'Happy are the sterile, the wombs that
never bore and the breasts that never nursed.' Then they will begin
saying to the mountains, 'Fall on us,' and to the hills, 'Cover us.' If
they do these things in the green wood, what will happen in the dry?"
(Lk 23, 26-31)

* * *

A BEGGAR

I too would be a beggar . . .

I too would be a beggar . . .

—but wealth of friendship attracts me so

—but abundance of praise fills my soul

—but rich foods must not be wasted

—but expensive coins bring security

—but a mansion protects from rain and foe

I too would be a beggar . . .

I too would be a beggar . . .

    —if only your eyes one day would meet mine

    —if only your voice could be heard in my silence

    —if only your arms, empty & lonely, might surround me

    —if only your feet might mark out my path

    —if only your heart within my breast would beat

I too would be a beggar . . .

I too would be a beggar . . .

    —and run free, not held by any string

    —and trouble all with love and concern

    —and stand apart in grace filled detachment

    —and sing a plaintive song of a distant home

    —and embrace the poor as sister and brother

I too would be a beggar . . .

I too would be a beggar . . .

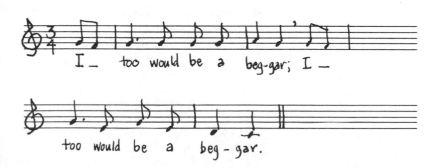

PRAYER

Lord-beggar Jesus, what would you have of me? My stingy soul and hardened heart fail to recognize you. My deep desires for comfort and security prevent me from following you. May I hear your "please" and see your tear-soiled cheek. May my dream to stand apart come true and may I know we stand together on every bleak corner of life—for you are there.

* * *

QUOTATIONS FROM JOHANNES B. METZ [6]

We are all beggars. We are all members of a species that is not sufficient unto itself. We are all creatures plagued by unending doubts and restless, unsatisfied hearts. Of all creatures, we are the poorest and the most incomplete. Our needs are always beyond our capacities, and we only find ourselves when we lose ourselves. (27)

* * *

God's fidelity to man is what gives man the courage to be true to himself. And the legacy of his total commitment to mankind, the proof of his fidelity to our poverty, is the cross. The cross is the sacrament of poverty of spirit, the sacrament of authentic humanness in a sinful world. It is the sign that one man remained true to his humanity, that he accepted it in full obedience. (19)

* * *

Christ, the sinless one, experienced the poverty of human existence more deeply and more excruciatingly than any other man could. He saw its many faces, including those shadowy aspects we never glimpse. In the poverty of his passion, he had no consolation, no companion angels, no guiding star, no Father in heaven. All he had was his own lonely heart, bravely facing its ordeal even as far as the cross. (18)

* * *

REFLECTION

Have you seen him? The pencil man, the blind man, the singer, the beggar! Perhaps on a street corner? Sad face, hopeless expression, disheveled hair! Just a voice that utters a pitiful "please." Empty hands and empty pockets! Troubler of the human heart! I saw him on 20th and G in the city of Washington, D.C. A ragged body wrapped in cardboard, lying on a grate, seeking some comfort from a cold autumn night. Several trees were already bare. Most birds had already moved farther south. Only the poor remained, hoping for some shelter in our nation's capital. I saw the bag lady coming out of a soup kitchen in Milwaukee. Her eyes retained a slight glow as they ventured into the city's darkness. Food yes, shelter no. What park bench, alleyway, or large culvert would welcome her that freezing March night? I saw the

I too would be a beggar

barefooted child in old Jerusalem. Running the streets and beseeching affluent tourists for a small coin, the abandoned child sought a bite to eat and a moment of compassion. The Holy City—one huge orphanage! I saw the locked corridor of the mental hospital. Some semblance of humanity gazed from partially-opened doors. Expressionless eyes and mumbling voices saddened attendants and infrequent visitors. And I . . . I saw . . .

* * *

COMMENTARY

A MENDICANT LORD

Jesus of Nazareth, Jesus of Calcutta, Jesus of Ethiopia, you are the mendicant of mendicants. I have struggled to know you over the years. The book of Hebrews, John's Gospel, Paul's epistles say much and yet you escape my grasp. My dusty theological tomes speak of ontological and existential characteristics of a God-made-man and yet my mind reels in confusion. Perhaps, perhaps it is in the world's poor—the bag lady, the crippled pencil man, the sightless musician on the street corner, perhaps they speak most powerfully of you. I long to know you, Jesus of this world. I long to know the movements of your heart and the vision of your mind. A divine mendicant? No wonder we are confused and perplexed!

A UBIQUITOUS MENDICANT

Like a shadow we cannot shake you, Jesus. You trail us in every place, at all times. Always and everywhere, relentlessly, your voice pierces our dumb world, your face is reflected in all lands so that even the blind must see. No matter whether I'm walking the streets or sitting in a room, you once again appear. Your whisper shouts and your presence pervades the parlor of my heart. Perhaps I can find a voice different from your plaintive "please"; perhaps I can find the key to lock out the sound of sadness. Still you come through cracks and crevices. Your voice will not be silenced, your face will not be hidden.

AN IMPLORING MENDICANT

Lord, so many coins I have wasted and continue to waste in the face of your begging. Only by blocking out your "tear-soiled cheek" can I purchase expensive food and entertainment; only by avoiding your hair matted in blood can I be extravagant in my purchases of cosmetics, clothes and jewelry. Our affluent stores attract us, like flies to honey, and then entrap us in false security. Teach us, Lord, to make fewer purchases. Help us to share our coins with the needy. May your imploring heart turn our stony hearts to flesh.

A DEMANDING MENDICANT

Giving up one sandwich does not satisfy your hunger. A single day's service does not quench your thirst. Whatever I give up does not quiet my conscience. Lord, are you a greedy beggar? Do you demand all and "force" us to empty our minds, hearts and purses into your outstretched hands? My pennies are too small, like my love. Your sorrowful gaze does not seek my purse but rather my heart. How can I empty that which itself is poor and barren? Master beggar, fill me with your compassion and then I will give all.

A RELENTLESS MENDICANT

Lord, you go so deep. Beyond coins and pennies you ask of us family and friends, lovers and children. You ask of us our very lives, our blood. Such divine imposition is hard to bear. No wonder that I offer you a one-way bus ticket so that your eyes and voice will be far from me. Your demands are so absolute, your pursuit so unrelenting. Only by focusing on your face, my beggar, can I possibly let go of my nearest and dearest, can I let go of the string holding my heart.

A FELLOW MENDICANT

You invite me to hit the streets. Enough of pondering and questioning—now is the time for action. My dream is two-fold: to be with you in a shared life—to participate in your mission of troubling people for their heart. My torment is deep and long. I wish to empty myself and visit the street corners of life. Come, master beggar, and give me the strength to stay with you on the journey.

Exile

MANTRA: **an exile out of heaven**

SOURCE: Jessica Powers' "Night of Storm"

The times are winter. Thus a poet signed
our frosty fate. Life is a night of snow.
Our faithless footprints from our own heels blow.
Where can an exile out of heaven go,
with murk and terror in a trackless place
and stinging bees swept down upon his face?
Or what is else? There is your world within.
And now the soul is supplicant: O most
wretched and blind, come home! Where love has been
burns the great lantern of the Holy Ghost.
Here in His light; review your world of frost:
a drifting miracle! What had been night
reels with unending eucharists of light.[7]

*   *   *

PARALLEL REFERENCES

For the man and his wife the Lord God made leather garments, with
which he clothed them. Then the Lord God said: "See! The man has
become like one of us, knowing what is good and what is bad! Therefore, he must not be allowed to put out his hand to take fruit from the
tree of life also, and thus eat of it and live forever." The Lord God
therefore banished him from the garden of Eden, to till the ground from
which he had been taken. When he expelled the man, he settled him

east of the garden of Eden; and he stationed the cherubim and the fiery
revolving sword to guard the way to the tree of life. (Genesis 3, 21-24)

> "The night comes on when no one can work.
> While I am in the world
> I am the light of the world."

With that Jesus spat on the ground, made mud with his saliva, and
smeared the man's eyes with the mud. Then he told him, "Go, wash in the
pool of Siloam." (This name means "One who has been sent.") So the man
went off and washed, and came back able to see. (John 9, 4b-7)

* * *

THE EXILE
> An exile out of heaven,
>
> An exile out of heaven:
>
>> —lost on the darkling plains
>>
>> —frozen by the bitter cold
>>
>> —battered by the merciless sleet
>>
>> —frost-bitten by the hostile snow
>>
>> —blinded by the murky night
>
> An exile out of heaven,
>
> An exile out of heaven:
>
>> —found by the lantern of love
>>
>> —warmed by the lamp's soft light
>>
>> —fondled by a friendly glance
>>
>> —healed by a memory of home
>>
>> —enlightened by a eucharistic flame
>
> An exile out of heaven,
>
> An exile out of heaven.

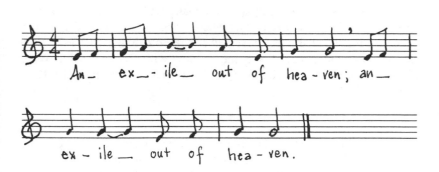

An — ex — - ile — out of hea - ven ; an —

ex - ile — out of hea - ven.

PRAYER

Veni, Creator Spiritus! Come, Holy Spirit! Fill our nights of terror and fear with faith in Jesus, the bearer of light and love. Shine the beam of the great lantern of your love on our hearts. Bring us from our exile to our home in your heart. As you dispel our darkness and destroy our winter, we shall live to warm our cold and fragile world with your love. Amen.

✦ ✦ ✦

QUOTATIONS FROM ST. PAUL[8]

Be imitators of me, my brothers [and sisters]. Take as your guide those who follow the example that we set. Unfortunately, many go about in a way which shows them to be enemies of the cross of Christ. I have often said this to you before; this time I say it with tears. Such as these will end in disaster! Their god is their belly and their glory is in their shame. I am talking about those who are set upon the things of this world. As you well know, we have our citizenship in heaven; it is from there that we eagerly await the coming of our Savior, the Lord Jesus Christ. He will give a new form to this lowly body of ours and remake it according to the pattern of his glorified body, by his power to subject everything to himself. (Philippians 3, 17-21)

* * *

Since we have been raised up in company with Christ, set your heart on what pertains to higher realms where Christ is seated at God's right hand. Be intent on things above rather than on things on earth. After all, you have died! Your life is hidden now with Christ in God. When Christ our life appears, then you shall appear with him in glory. (Colossians 3, 1-4)

* * *

Yes, we know that all creation groans and is in agony even until now. Not only that, but we ourselves, although we have the Spirit as first fruits, groan inwardly while we await the redemption of our bodies. In hope we were saved. But hope is not hope if its object is seen; how is it possible for one to hope for what he sees? And hoping for what we cannot see means awaiting it with patient endurance. (Romans 8, 23-25)

* * *

REFLECTION

Fiction provides us with stories of exiles and homecomings, of despair and hope, of darkness and light, of winters and springs. Fictitious characters are members of the human family and, as such, have insights and feelings to share that assist us on our pilgrim journey. Several come to mind. In Shakespeare's "The Merchant of Venice," Portia says to her maid as they walk in the darkness:

"That light we see is burning in my hall.
How far that little candle throws its beams!
So shines a good deed in a naughty world." (v, i, 89-91)

Our world is naughty. Evil is too present and manifest. Yet the darkness is pierced with the light of millions of good deeds. The letter asking forgiveness, the stranger given shelter, the trembling child held in a mother's embrace; the hand of the dying feeling the peace of presence. The great lantern of love burns in little but powerful ways.

Charles Dickens begins his story, *The Tale of Two Cities*, with a reflection on the historical situation of 1775: "It was the best of times, it was the worst of times, it was the age of wisdom, it was the age of foolishness, it was the epoch of belief, it was the epoch of incredulity, it was the season of darkness, it was the spring of hope, it was the winter of despair, we had everything before us, we had nothing before us, we were all going direct to Heaven, we were all going direct the other way—in short, the period was so far like the present period, that some of its noisiest authorities insisted on its being received, for good or for evil, in the superlative degree of comparison only." The seasons come and go. Yet for the exile, we who travel outside our natural home, winter is always in the air. Only through faith is there an inner space of light and warmth. A peace of presence sustains us and offers hope.

John Singer, the deaf-mute in Carson McCullers' powerful novel *The Heart is a Lonely Hunter*, comments about the people who circle his life:

> They are all very busy people. In fact they are so busy that it will be hard for you to picture them. I do not mean they work at their jobs all day and night but that they have much business in their minds always that does not let them rest. They come up to my room and talk to me until I do not understand how a person can open and shut his or her mouth so much without being weary. However, the New York Cafe owner is different—he is not just like the others. He has a very black beard so that he has to shave twice daily, and he owns one of these electric razors. He watches. The others all have something they hate. And they all have something they love more than eating or sleeping or wine or friendly company. That is why they are always so busy. (New York: Bantam Books, 1940, pp. 182-183)

So much of life is missed because of a failure to be present to the moment. The lantern is not noticed; our exile only deepens.

In an antiphon in honor of Mary, the Church offers a reflection on our journey: "To you do we send up our sighs, mourning and weeping in this vale of tears. Turn then, most gracious advocate, your eyes of mercy towards us, and after this exile show to us the blessed fruit of your womb, Jesus." This song contains a perspective offering us aspects of our identity and destiny. It casts forth a beam that lights our path. A future home awaits us and there is no ultimate resting point on earth. A failure to come to this knowledge leaves us in a meaningless void.

* * *

COMMENTARY

LIFE

Lord, what is life? Is it a night of snow, a blizzard ending in a frosty fate? Are all our days to be deprived of spring and summer? The terror of nuclear death has settled in our hearts; the gloom of holocausts and indiscriminate violence has cast its shadow over the pages of our history and daily tabloids. Surely the night of snow must yield to the spring dawn; surely some ray of hope can dispel our universal despair. How strange for a poet to sign a document lettered in dread. Is this not the work of some disconnected existential philosopher? But a poet! That messenger sent to expand, not contract the heart. Yet the poet sees, sees that much of our times is indeed winter. To sign any other document would be false.

It was in a garden called Gethsemane that you felt so strongly the winter's chill. In the darkness you prayed alone over a fate you dreaded. In aloneness, no human friend came to support you. A night of snow pressed hard upon your heart and only the heat of your love provided sufficient warmth to make it through the sea of cold hearts surrounding you. Teach us, Lord Jesus, to endure the winters of our life. Strengthen us to venture into the frigid life-zones of our sisters and brothers that they might experience your warmth. Point out a path, a path of peace, so that all might see your face and find in you a haven from the tempest.

EXILE

Lord, we walk and stumble east of Eden. Surely there must be some space we call home, some path that is well-worn and comfortable. These are not to be found. Rather, as we blindly journey on, panic from within and fear from without take all comfort away. Where, oh where can we go? From village to village you wandered. Nazareth was no longer home and thus you journeyed to the Jordan, then on to Jericho and Naim, Capernaum and Cana—and finally Jerusalem. A divine exile walking the human valley. Even the table of Martha and the rapt gaze of Mary could not still your longing for home. Nothing but the Father's will could bring peace. Still our terrors, Lord. We are fragile pilgrims who keep too busy and pretend much of the time. Protect us against the sleet of rejection and the stinging indifference of nature. In our homelessness, journey with us lest we lose heart. Give us courage in the darkness.

HOME

Gracious Lord, draw us deep within, beyond our greed and envy, our fears and angers. Show us that inner sanctuary where you alone dwell. There we touch your grace and receive our sight. There, deep within, we are nourished so abundantly that we yearn to share with others. Only by means of the inner journey can we experience your mercy and hope. Do not let us remain strangers to ourselves; end our exile by calling us home. Early dawn found you in prayer. Leaving the sleeping disciples behind, you found a quiet place for solitary communication with the Father. From deep inner recesses flowed stories of sparrows and lilies of the field, sheep and goats in eternal separation, a dream of a harvest come home. In the quiet mornings the world within stilled the storm of apathy and hatred that you met on the road. In prayer you found intimacy with the Father and all creation. Our culture has few resources to construct an inner cartography. Our maps draw us to a life of action. Even the first set of rooms in the interior castle remain vacant. Lord, empower our heart to trust in the mystery of your love and intimacy. Dispel our reluctance and grace us with confidence. Send your Spirit into our lives.

THE GREAT LANTERN

Lumen Christi! Your Church sings out your song. Love itself has entered our world: sins are forgiven, broken hearts mended, the lost are found. A great lantern burns in a dark manger. A light breaks forth for Zachariah in the temple. The darkness of sin is scattered for an adulterous woman. In your warmth, Lord, our icy hearts melt and we experience resurrection.

Near Emmaus a night was turned into day. As bread was broken, love and knowledge filled the hearts of the two disciples. A great lantern burned, never to be extinguished. Bread would continue through the generations to be taken, blessed, broken and given for all in need. Darkness and doubt lost their sting. A miracle of thanksgiving filled the world. Jesus, shed your light upon us. In the light of your mercy help us recall the memories of your healing presence. In the light of your compassion, help us to enter the pain and joy of our brothers and sisters. In the light of your love, help us to trust your word and to do it with loving obedience.

Wilderness

MANTRA: **there were winters in his heart**

SOURCE: Jessica Powers' "About Bruno"

Saint Bruno's gift was his uninterrupted
conversation with God.

How did this wonder come to him? Without
Carthusian insights I can only guess:
there must have been at first some seeds of grace
which Bruno planted in his wilderness.
He must have watered them with tears, and kept
his little garden friendly to the sun
till the shoots came and, marvelously, flowers.
(Words were his flowers, to woo the Holy One.)
Bruno had peace, I know, but all the same
I doubt that he perceived if answers came.

And surely there were winters in his heart
when leaf and blossom died, and the land froze,
and a white silence covered everything.
He offered God this silence, I suppose,
and his cold poverty (which few believe
that God in His warm silence will receive).

How did this wonder come at last to him?
I would surmise: when Bruno understood
how love that crushed him had no gift for God—
though through all seasons he had sought the good—
he entered his own hut, pulled down the shades,
and sat and grappled with his pain till he

29

himself became the word, the total need,
the gift, the outcry, the last agony.
And one day God, most ready to discover
the moment that a heart fills to the brim,
burst into Bruno's time, sat down beside him,
and eager with delight gave to this lover
the joy of endless dialogue with Him.[9]

* * *

PARALLEL REFERENCES

Then King David went in and sat before the Lord and said, "Who
am I, Lord God, and who are the members of my house, that you have
brought me to this point? Yet even this you see as too little, Lord God;
you have also spoken of the house of your servant for a long time to
come: this too you have shown to man, Lord God! What more can
David say to you? You know your servant, Lord God! For your
servant's sake and as you have had at heart, you have brought about
this entire magnificent disclosure to your servant. And so—

"Great are you, Lord God! There is none like you and there is no
God but you, just as we have heard it told. What other nation on earth
is there like your people Israel, which God has led, redeeming it as his
people; so that you have made yourself renowned by doing this magnificent deed." (2 Samuel 7, 18-23a)

* * *

Then he [Jesus] went out and made his way, as was his custom, to
the Mount of Olives; his disciples accompanied him. On reaching the
place he said to them, "Pray that you may not be put to the test." He
withdrew from them about a stone's throw, then went down on his
knees and prayed in these words: "Father, if it is your will, take this
cup from me; yet not my will but yours be done." An angel then appeared to him from heaven to strengthen him. In his anguish he prayed
with all the greater intensity, and his sweat became like drops of blood
falling to the ground. Then he rose from prayer and came to his disci-

ples, only to find them asleep, exhausted with grief. He said to them, "Why are you sleeping? Wake up, and pray that you may not be subjected to the trial." (Luke 22, 39-46)

* * *

WINTER SILENCE

there were winters in his heart
there were winters in his heart

the sun a stranger
there were winters in his heart

the night, an empty cradle

* * *

the stars—distant companions
he offered God his silence

the journey—alone

* * *

no silver, no gold
he offered God his silence

no honor, no trust

* * *

no flowers sown here
there were winters in his heart

yet hope with the dawn

* * *

there were winters in his heart,
there were winters in his heart.

There were win___-ters in his heart; there were

win___-ters in his heart.

PRAYER

Lord, onto the frozen tundras of our souls, bring the warmth of your love, the fire of your presence. We offer you our cold poverty and humble silence; we await your coming to dine with us again. And if the winter silence is not to be broken, enkindle a spark of hope deep within our souls. In Jesus' name we pray.

* * *

QUOTATIONS FROM THOMAS MERTON[10]

And though it is certain that we must speak if and when we can, silence is always more important. The crises of the age are so enormous and the mystery of evil so unfathomable: the action of well-meaning men is so absurd and tends so much to contribute to the very evils it tries to overcome: all these things should show us that the real way is prayer, and penance, and closeness to God in poverty and solitude. (20)

* * *

I believe my vocation is essentially that of a pilgrim and an exile in life, that I have no proper place in this world but that for that reason I am in some sense to be the friend and brother of people everywhere, especially those who are exiles and pilgrims like myself . . . My life is in many ways simple, but it is also a mystery which I do not attempt to really understand, as though I were led by the hand in a night where I see nothing, but can fully depend on the Love and Protection of Him Who guides me. (52)

* * *

The reality that is present to us and in us: call it Being, call it Atman, call it Pneuma . . . or Silence. And the simple fact that by being attentive, by learning to listen (or recovering the natural capacity to listen which cannot be learned any more than breathing), we can find ourself engulfed in such happiness that it cannot be explained: the happiness of being at one with everything in that hidden ground of Love for which there can be no explanations. (115)

The long hours of silence are the best thing in the world and I appreciate them more than I can say. (153)

REFLECTION

It was in the early years of high school that I first experienced the power and mystery of internal dialogue. An English teacher assigned us unsophisticated sophomores some autobiographical readings. In these frank and personal journals I was amazed to hear the accounts of the richness of people's lives and to realize that at certain moments I too had similar experiences. In these readings an interior dialogue was going on: individuals raising and answering questions deep within their own hearts. Dialogue assumes presence. We can speak to our hearts of some past memory, to our minds of some reoccurring question, to our souls of the mystery of life and death. Our dialogue ranges further to include, at times, a classmate, a friend, indeed, our God. Dialogue is one means of making connection between our isolated self and the rest of reality.

What is the possibility of an uninterrupted dialogue on the busy and distracting journey of life? Was Bruno's gift a permanent grace or one that proved transitory? Is it possible, indeed desirable, to strive for such a dialogue since it might endanger our being present to the moment: attending to a dying patient, flying a jumbo jet across the Atlantic, teaching Kant's "categorical imperative." Can one carry on a dual dialogue with a resident guest as well as with the events of everyday life? The sun offers us a clue. Just as our life-giving star communicates warmth and light to the entire planet, we can respond with an uninterrupted act of gratitude for these blessings. That act is intentional and perduring even though we may be busy with life's affairs. Though not at the forefront of our consciousness, the grateful sun-worshipper has an abiding awareness which comes into focus at specific times (most likely at dawn and dusk). By way of analogy, the faith-filled person comes to an awareness of God's redeeming love being always present. That consciousness leads to an uninterrupted act of gratitude. A final observation: in the winter the sun seems shy and does not want to spend so much time with us. On cloudy days, we might even feel rejected. Then at night, it totally vanishes and one might wonder if it still exists. Yet the sun has a constancy that winter, night and clouds cannot alter. Religious faith assures us that God is faithful and always present. That faith fact allows for the possibility and power of an interrupted dialogue. Bruno lived in that kind of perduring faith.

* * *

COMMENTARY

BRUNO'S WILDERNESS

And in the desert a blossom will bloom. Our souls are not unlike the desert: thirsty, frequently deserted, hungering for physical, human and divine nourishment. Seeds of grace, watered by our tears and warmed by the sun, germinate and share their life and beauty with the world. But before that happens there are seasons of loneliness and doubt that cause the spirit to tremble. Buried seeds need deep faith and hope. They need the warmth of love to draw them forth. Perseverance is a special grace needed when answers do not come. This virtue allows us to utter words of petition to God who appears so distant. Our wooing words, like small shoots, entice the Lord to come and begin to transform the hardness of our arid land into a fertile field. Tears soften the soil and provide the necessary moisture for our thirsty hearts. As we offer God our symbols of affection and desire, a divine refrain returns again and again to nurture our feeble efforts. And spring with its blossoms comes again.

BRUNO'S WINTERS

Here in northern Wisconsin winters are fairly predictable. Frozen lakes, mountains of snow, howling blizzards and barren trees tell the tale of winter's harshness. A white silence blankets the day and shrouds the night; we acknowledge a "cold poverty" that deprives us of warm breezes and the lush richness of nature. Desolate too are the winters of the human spirit. Lifeless and cold, we are tempted to despair. Does not Scripture tell us that "by their fruits you shall know them"? No fruits? Then I'm a nobody! How could God receive a cold poverty, a white silence, a dormant field, a fragile heart, a sinful life? Scripture also says: "When I am weak then I am strong." God embraces our emptiness and brokenness with his love. We must believe that "God in his warm silence" hears the fall of every tear and the whisper of every sigh.

BRUNO'S HUT

In our inner sanctuary we stand alone. Here, not the distorting circus mirror, but the mirror of honesty, the honest mirror, reflects back to us our nakedness and pain. In the solitude of contemplation comes the awareness that God is not after our words or our dreams, our achievements or our successes, our failures or our sins. God longs for our very selves. We are to become the gift. No longer can we hide behind the words of philosophers or theologians, behind our physical or psychological needs, behind the outcries of injustice, behind the agony of lost loves. All of this falls to the floor and is swept away. In our hut we stand alone before the mystery of God, and then we kneel. Having no gift but ourselves for a loving God is a searing pain. It seems to speak of ingratitude; it smacks of inadequacy. It has the ring of a wasted life or one too colored by failure. Attempts to do good are on the record, cannot be denied, but these stumblings have not amounted to much. What weighs so heavily is that we review all of this— this poorly-lived life—in the face of God's tremendous love. "What return can I make to the Lord for all the good that he has done for me?" That is our painful and eternal question.

BRUNO'S TIME

"*Kairos*" is the term used to express God's time, those special moments of grace. In contrast to "*chronos*" (chronology) which speaks of daily seconds, minutes and hours, "*kairos*" is the intrusion of grace into human history. When a heart is properly disposed and filled to the brim with desire and longing, God bursts through to dwell in us in a special way. And he comes to stay—as long as we offer him hospitality.

And then the dialogue begins. No inflection is missed, no intimation goes unnoticed, no stirring undetected. In mutual delight and joy, conversation is shared. In this friendship of love all is open for discussion. But the dialogue is not limited to listening and speaking—it leads to silent understandings and surrender. With a final plunge into the cool depths of obedience, the never-ending love-dialogue overflows into committed discipleship and the building of the kingdom.

Love

MANTRA: **with a penny match of love**

SOURCE: Jessica Powers' "This Paltry Love"

I love you, God, with a penny match of love
that I strike when the big and bullying dark of need
chases my startled sunset over the hills
and in the walls of my house small terrors move.
It is the sight of this paltry love that fills
my deepest pits with seething purgatory,
that thus I love you, God—*God*— who would sow
my heights and depths with recklessness of glory,
who hold back light-oceans straining to spill on me, on *me*,
stifling here in the dungeon of my ill.
This puny spark I scorn, I who had dreamed
of fire that would race to land's end, shouting your worth,
of sun that would fall to earth with a mortal wound
and rise and run, streaming with light like blood,
splattering the sky,
soaking the ocean itself, and all the earth.[11]

* * *

PARALLEL REFERENCES

Turning to the woman, he [Jesus] said to Simon: "You see this woman? I came to your home and you provided me with no water for my feet. She has washed my feet with her tears and wiped them with her hair. You gave me no kiss, but she has not ceased kissing my feet since I entered. You did not anoint my head with oil, but she has anointed my feet with perfume. I tell you, that is why her many sins are forgiven—because of her great love. Little is forgiven the one whose love is small." (Luke 7, 44-47)

* * *

Love, then, consists in this:
not that we have loved God
but that he has loved us
and has sent his Son as an offering for our sins.
Beloved, if God has loved us so,
we must have the same love for one another. (1 John 4, 10-11)

* * *

I LOVE YOU, GOD

    With a penny match of love,
    with a penny match of love.

                i love you, god
   —no eternal flame warming the hearts of the frozen
   —no brilliant torch shattering the darkness of fear
   —no roaring bonfire chasing arrogant autumnal ghosts
   —no blazing log driving the frost back to the north
   —no galloping forest fire consuming hill and valley

    i love you, god

* * *

    with a penny match of love,
    with a penny match of love.

                i love you, god
   —a small quivering in the vastness of the night
   —a fragile flicker in the winds of war
   —a desolate spark tiptoeing on the edge of despair
   —a frail dim taper in a wrinkled hand
   —a humble candle of imperfect wax

    i love you, god

with a penny match of love,
with a penny match of love.

                                        i love you, god
   —not like your sunburst of forgiveness
   —not like your jubilant "recklessness of glory"
   —not like your splattered brilliance of a divine sunset
   —not like your "light-oceans" of hope
   —not like your charged grandeur of a faith-filled dawn

   i love you, god

with a penny match of love
with a penny match of love.

PRAYER

Lord, the brilliant fire of your love consumes the dampness of sin. Like late autumn logs we seek to be ignited by your touch, enkindled by your sight, ablaze with the sound of your voice. Send your Pentecost Spirit upon us and we shall renew the face and heart of the earth with your love.

* * *

QUOTATIONS FROM HANS URS VON BALTHASAR[12]

This drama [Jesus' death and resurrection], in which God's design for the world is realized, in which all the individual meanings contained in nature and the human world are accomplished—that is, in that mode of transcendence we spoke of above—this drama is an act and a manifestation of an eternal and boundless love. But this love, far from being a universally-pervading medium in which everything dissolves in a vague emotionalism, is shown in a clearly-delineated figure, occupying a definite place in history (in no other way can the personality of the Father appear in the world), taking visible form in distinct words, acts, sufferings and miracles. Consequently every beginning of love that reaches out from the world towards God must let itself be transformed and integrated into the drama of this unique Person, so as, in him, to penetrate to heaven itself (Heb. IX. 25)—that is to say, to be delivered from the dim colorlessness of all that is merely of this world, and take on a splendour of its own, worthy to stand alongside that of God himself. (46-47)

* * *

With a pen-ny match of love; with a pen-ny match of love.

Love is the content and aim of contemplation, and so, from the outset, should be directly sought and realized. Love desires the presence of the beloved, and so the person praying places himself in God's presence; or rather he realizes in his spirit the truth that God has long since placed him in his own presence in a special manner. Nothing stands between him and the eternal love; there is no need of a mediator in the case of a single being (Gal. III. 20). All that occurs in contemplation is contained in the framework of this presence. All that I hear of God's word, the insights and joys I find in it by God's grace, the praise of God and what I gain from it, all derives meaning from love, and is the fruit of mutual presence and immanence. (104-105)

* * *

Christian love always establishes truth between two or more persons, and that truth is ultimately Christ who dwells in the midst of those gathered together in his name (Mt. XVIII. 20). Love is thus seen to be the ground, the medium and the end of all the sacraments and all that the Church does to lead men into the truth; for sacraments and teaching are both an initiation into the reality consisting of man's participation in God's love, which has all the qualities enumerated by St. Paul in his hymn to charity (1 Cor, XIII) (172)

* * *

REFLECTION

It happened sporadically and yet with a strange pattern. I speak of my encounters with Elizabeth Barrett Browning (1806-1861) and her famous Sonnet 43:

How do I love thee? Let me count the ways.
I love thee to the depth and breadth and height
My soul can reach, when feeling out of sight
For the ends of Being and ideal Grace.
I love thee to the level of everyday's
Most quiet need, by sun and candle-light.
I love thee freely, as men strive for Right;

I love thee purely, as they turn from Praise.
I love thee with the passion put to use
In my old griefs, and with my childhood's faith.
I love thee with a love I seemed to lose
With my lost saints—I love thee with the breath,
Smiles, tears, of all my life!—and, if God choose,
I shall but love thee better after death.

My first experience of this verse was in eighth grade, a second as a senior in high school, then in second-year theology. Now, of its own free will, the sonnet revisits my heart with great frequency.

No paltry love in this sonnet, no penny match of love. Indeed the love of which Browning speaks is ablaze and passionate. Specific analogies are used to attempt to describe the intensity of such human affection. One wonders how long it could be sustained. One wonders if it is too romantic in its substance.

Cardinal Newman once wrote that he would not give much for a love that was not extravagant: "I would not give much for that love which is never extravagant, which always observes the proprieties. . . What mother, what husband or wife, what youth or maiden in love, but says a thousand foolish things, in a way of endearment, which the speaker would be sorry for strangers to hear; yet they are not on that account unwelcome to the parties to whom they are addressed." We hold in admiration intensity of life and love and flee from the paltry as unworthy of the human spirit. Fullness of life and nothing else is the desired order of the day. In reading Jessica Powers' "This Paltry Love" and Elizabeth Barrett Browning's sonnet side by side, a strange sensation arises within me. While the latter selection appeals to my dreams, it is the former that presses upon me the reality of the human condition. Regardless, we need both to motivate us on life's journey. I think it was George Herbert who once wrote that a love and a cough cannot be concealed. A penny match of love, for all its smallness, might be a consolation to many of us who have only this to give. And it will not be concealed. In its own finite ways, that match shares what it has.

Perhaps its humble task is to empower others and be a catalyst to transform the world.

* * *

COMMENTARY

A PENNY MATCH

The poet's question "How do I love thee? Let me count the ways" is only appropriate in the presence of extravagant love. Embarrassing beyond words is this interrogation to those who know how limited and small their affection is—a mere "penny match of love." And yet, even a match casts some light and warmth. No love, regardless of its size or shape, should be unnoticed or left unencouraged. At certain times this small love becomes active. When the calm and beauty of a sunset, startled from behind by needs that loom large with meaning, takes off over the hills to the dark west, then we are thrown out of the largeness of nature into the narrow confines of our own dwelling. Here the closets of fears and terrors are jarred open and have the appearance of immensity because of the dark. Such an experience threatens our meager love with extinction

SEETHING PURGATORY

Mirrors are ambivalent creatures. Joy flows when the glass reflects back moments of glory; deep sorrow when we are told of our smallness and inadequacies. That sorrow turns into seething purgatory because of the contrast between the recklessness of God's glory and the puniness of our cramped loves. The shame of it all is overwhelming. Herein lies a strange truth: it is the saint who is incessantly and painfully aware that as life progresses, so too does the sense of one's own sinfulness. Sin here is felt as the gap between God's infinite love and the meagerness of human finite response. Sin is not so much a matter of commission or omission. Rather, it is a purgatorial sensitivity that we are unable to outrun God's love and the gap continually increases. No wonder that we stifle in the dungeon of our illness.

DREAM

Our penny match of love—that puny spark—is held in contempt. An ancient dream must be re-ignited. Sent to enkindle our land, we imagine a world filled with the fire of the Holy Spirit, a world in which the sin of God's glory will splatter the sky and soak the ocean and all creation with its beauty. A light for all nations will come and all darkness will be scattered. Is such a dream an illusion? Is it possible that our small and impotent love can blaze anew and re-create the world? Only one solution emerges in this dilemma: our paltry love must be joined to the love that Christ has for the Father. Our puny spark must attach itself to the Pentecost flame that turned cowardice into courage. Our terrors must be placed at the feet of a trustworthy Father who longs for our salvation. Only then will these chains that hold us in our dungeons be broken and we will be set free.

Suffering

MANTRA: **the great gift of suffering**

SOURCE: Jessica Powers' "The Sign of the Cross"

The lovers of Christ lift out their hands to
the great gift of suffering.
For how could they seek to be warmed and clothed
and delicately fed,
to wallow in praise and to drink deep draughts
of an undeserved affection,
have castle for home and a silken couch for bed,
when He the worthy went forth, wounded and hated,
and grudged of even a place to lay His head?

This is the badge of the filends of the Man of Sorrows:
the mark of the cross, faint replica of His,
become ubiquitous now; it spreads like a wild blossom
on the mountains of time and in each of the crevices.
Oh, seek that land where it grows in a rich abundance
with its thorny stem and its scent like bitter wine,
for wherever Christ walks He casts its seed
and He scatters its purple petals.
It is the flower of His marked elect, and the fruit
it bears is divine.

Choose it, my heart. It is a beautiful sign.[13]

* * *

45

PARALLEL REFERENCES

But those things I used to consider gain I have now reappraised as loss in the light of Christ. I have come to rate all as loss in the light of the surpassing knowledge of my Lord Jesus Christ. For his sake I have forfeited everything; I have accounted all else rubbish so that Christ may be my wealth and I may be in him, not having any justice of my own based on observance of the law. The justice I possess is that which comes through faith in Christ. It has its origin in God and is based on faith. I wish to know Christ and the power flowing from his resurrection; likewise to know how to share in his sufferings by being formed into the pattern of his death. Thus do I hope that I may arrive at resurrection from the dead. (Philippians 3, 7-11)

* * *

Do not be surprised, beloved, that a trial by fire is occurring in your midst. It is a test for you, but it should not catch you off guard. Rejoice instead, in the measure that you share Christ's suffering. When his glory is revealed, you will rejoice exultantly. (1 Peter 4, 12-13)

* * *

THE SIGN OF THE CROSS
> the great gift of suffering,
> the great gift of suffering . . .

> great gifts ? ? ? ? ? ? ? ? ? ?
> —warmth in the cold tundras of our souls
> —clothes against the nakedness of shame
> —food in our seasons of starvation
> —praise from those we esteem worthy
> —affection to still the sting of loneliness
> —castles to house our bodies and our souls
> —beds of silk for morning comfort
> great gifts ? ? ? ? ? ? ? ? ? ?
> —wild blossoms of darkening doubt
> —thorny stems of painful rejection

—bitter wine of senseless hatred
—scattered seeds of restless fears
—purple petals of blood-stained beauty

The great gift of suffering,
The great gift of suffering.

PRAYER

Lord Jesus, you are the man of sorrows who invites us to be your disciples. Enable us to choose your mark, your badge, your flower of suffering. We seek other paths that exclude hurt and pain. Send your Spirit to make us lovers of your way that we may bear fruit that will last forever.

the great gift of suffering

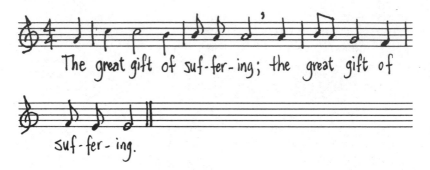

The great gift of suf-fer-ing; the great gift of suf-fer-ing.

QUOTATIONS FROM DOUGLAS STEERE[14]

For Christian saints are sons [and daughters] of One who made the cross a symbol of victory. St. Lawrence as he lay dying refused the offer of a mattress, saying, "My Saviour died not on a feather-bed but on the hard wood of the cross," and this temper, to take what comes without softening it for themselves, marks these men and women throughout Christian history. (46)

* * *

Now, an "apostle" is not an apostle by reason of any inherited characteristic either of physique, intelligence, will, emotion, psychological type, or abnormal faculty of mystical apprehension. He is an apostle only as whatever capacities he possesses are wholly open to use for the purposes of God. He is an apostle by reason of the totality of his abandonment to God. He is an apostle because the supernatural world that impinges upon the natural has become real enough to reckon on in every calculation of life. An apostle is "just a human being released from the love of self and enslaved by the love of God," and he rejoices in it. The life of an apostle is one where "God and His eternal order have more and more their undivided sway." (67)

* * *

Cromwell cried out again and again, "It is a terrible thing to fall into the hands of the living God." For the customary ambitions, expectations, and wise precautions, the lives of the apostles as we see them all bear witness to the shattering and scarification and kneading and rekneading of the life that goes on. An apostle must be teachable. There is death to be dealt to vast areas of claimfulness in the apostle's life. Yet where there is no death there can be no resurrection. (84)

* * *

REFLECTION

The oncologist told my friend that the bone cancer had begun to spread throughout his body. The pain would become increasingly severe but there was medication to alleviate much of the physical suffering. The gentle, honest doctor knew that no pills or therapy would ease the psychological or spiritual agony that followed upon this news. Suffering comes in many forms. Most often it is thrust upon us to our great consternation. Other times it advances as part of daily life in the small and not so small losses, in the unexpected failures, in psychological hurts. These unavoidable sufferings are in sharp contrast to suffering voluntarily chosen or received as a gift.

In *The Divine Milieu*, Teilhard de Chardin emphatically addresses the Christian attitude toward physical evil and articulates our duty in this regard: "To struggle against evil and to reduce to a minimum even the ordinary physical evil which threatens us, is unquestionably the first act of our Father who is in heaven; it would be impossible to conceive him in any other way, and still more impossible to love him." (84) There can be only one healthy way for people to extend their hands to suffering and to consider it a gift: suffering must be perceived as a means of identifying with the life of Jesus and sharing in the depth of his love. Suffering, imaged on the cross and as a flower whose fruit is divine, leads to a bonding with the Man of Sorrows who transforms sufferings into joys. Embracing suffering in this way is not at all sadistic. Further, Suffering embraced this way cannot be understood by the mind since it is a matter of the heart, a matter of love and identification. Later in the day my friend with the bone cancer reflected on his situation. "You know, this is a moment of grace for me. I just hope that I will be able to keep my eyes fixed on the Lord during this trial. Then all will be well."

* * *

COMMENTARY

LOVERS OF CHRIST

"Do you love me?" Peter had to search the depths of his heart for an honest response to the Lord's question. But not only Peter. That same question echoes down the centuries and each of us is addressed by God, through Christ, with the very same question. Evidence of some sort must be provided if indeed we are truly Christians. Lovers of Christ are a special breed who wear a special sign and have a distinctive life-style.

GIFT OF SUFFERING

Two surprises disturb our expectations: that lovers of Christ embrace suffering as proof of their identity and that suffering itself is a gift, a form of grace. Resistance to both physical and psychological suffering will be strong. The body dreads pain and our psyches avoid and flee from displeasures of any sort. Yet Christ was the suffering servant and no one can be with him, body and soul, without walking the same path. Suffering, in and of itself, is not sought or desired. Rather, since suffering gives entrance into union with God and companionship with Jesus, it is one of the great gifts of life. Again suffering is not an end but a means. A non-suffering life or a life devoted to sheer pleasure keeps us far from knowledge and love of the Lord. Such paths simply mean that we are lovers of self and seek superficial consolation.

DESIRES OF BODY AND SOUL

Strong are the desires for warmth and fine garments, rich foods and mellow wines, praise of friends and the larger public, affection and recognition from others, fine dwellings and soft beds. Our comfort zones are many. They attempt to ward off all forms of suffering and protect us from too much reality. Satiated we lack passion, laden with things we lack mobility, crowded with affection we lack a space for our God.

Jesus walked a different road. He chose the spiritual gait of poverty and emptiness. Wounded by word and blows, he used no violence.

Hated out of fear and dread, he returned no evil. Deprived of home and family, he took to himself the earth and all people. Jesus embraced suffering as a way of life because he was a person of compassion and love. No other choice would bring freedom to the people or union with his Father.

BADGE OF FRIENDSHIP

Friendship seeks a symbol. Married couples exchange rings in an attempt to speak of their mutual love and fidelity. Friendship with Christ has but one symbol: the cross. This confers unmistakable identity on the true disciple. Though many are baptized in Christ, their lives remain unmarked by the cross. Sacramental marking, be it through baptism, confirmation or anointing, is not sufficient. Daily life, not just liturgical celebrations, must characterize the embracing of the cross. Faint as the replica may be, we are invited to plunge into the experience of Christ, the man of sorrows. His suffering must become our own, and that by a free choice.

Homelessness

MANTRA: **loneliness of mystery**

SOURCE: Jessica Powers' "There is a Homelessness"

There is a homelessness, never to be clearly defined.
It is more than having no place of one's own,
   no bed or chair.
It is more than walking in a waste of wind,
or gleaning the crumbs where someone else has dined,
or taking a coin for food or clothes to wear.
The loan of things and the denial of things are possible to bear.

It is more, even, than homelessness of heart,
of being always a stranger at love's side,
of creeping up to a door only to start
at a shrill voice and to plunge back to the wide
dark of one's own obscurity and hide.

It is the homelessness of the soul in the body sown;
it is the loneliness of mystery:
of seeing oneself a leaf, inexplicable and unknown,
cast from an unimaginable tree;
of knowing one's life to be a brief wind blown
down a fissure of time in the rock of eternity.
The artist weeps to wrench this grief from stone;
he pushes his hands through the tangled vines of music,
   but he cannot set it free.

It is the pain of the mystic suddenly thrown
back from the noon of God to the night of his own humanity.
It is his grief; it is the grief of all those praying

in finite words to an Infinity
Whom, if they saw, they could not comprehend;
Whom they cannot see.[15]

* * *

PARALLEL REFERENCES

As they were making their way along, someone said to him, "I will be your follower wherever you go." Jesus said to him, "The foxes have lairs, the birds of the sky have nests, but the Son of Man has nowhere to lay his head." (Luke 9, 57-58)

* * *

Naomi said to her two daughters-in-law, "Go back, each of you, to your mother's house! May the Lord be kind to you as you were to the departed and to me! May the Lord grant each of you a husband and a home in which you will find rest." She kissed them good-by, but they wept with loud sobs, and told her they would return with her to her people. "Go back, my daughters!" said Naomi. "Why should you come with me? Have I other sons in my womb who may become your husbands? Go back my daughters! Go, for I am too old to marry again. And even if I could offer any hopes, or if tonight I had a husband or had borne sons, would you then wait and deprive yourselves of husbands until those sons grew up? No, my daughters! My lot is too bitter for you, because the Lord has extended his hand against me." Again they sobbed aloud and wept; and Orpah kissed her mother-in-law goodbye, but Ruth stayed with her. (Ruth 1, 8-14)

* * *

LONELINESS OF MYSTERY

loneliness of mystery,
loneliness of mystery . . .

perched alongside the ocean's immensity,
catching a glimpse of a moonlit spider's web,
tracking the fall of a drunken autumn leaf,

noting the flight of an early morning hawk,
trembling before the gaze of love,

> loneliness of mystery . . .
> loneliness of mystery . . .

crushed by the pain of a dying friend,
overwhelmed by the beauty of a single rose,
astonished at the tender mercy so tenderly given,
awed by the gracious acceptance of sufferings,
broken in the crucible of betrayed friendship.

loneliness of mystery . . .
loneliness of mystery . . .

PRAYER

God of mystery, may we enter your loneliness and listen to your heart. May we share in the fullness of life—its joys and sorrows, its ecstasies and agonies, its bondings and loneliness. May we keep "the vigil of mystery" and thus come to know and love you. Give us the courage to live, to die and to rise with you. Amen.

* * *

QUOTES FROM RAINER MARIA RILKE[16]

And all those people, men and women, who are in some transition, perhaps from madness to healing, perhaps also toward insanity; all with something infinitely fine in their faces, with a love, a knowledge, a joy, as with a light that is burning only a very little bit troubled and uneasy and could certainly be made clear again if someone would look and help. . . . But there is no one to help. No one to help those who are only just a very little bit perplexed, frightened, and intimidated; those who are just beginning to read things differently from the way they are meant; those who are still living in quite the same world, only that they walk just a little obliquely and therefore sometimes think that things are hanging over them; those who aren't at home in cities and lose themselves in them as in an evil wood without end—; all those to whom pain is happening every day, all those who can no longer hear their wills going in the noise, all those over whom fear has grown,—why does no one help them in the big cities?

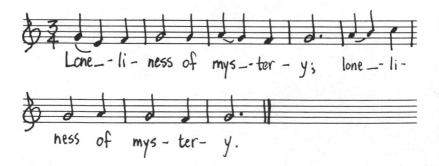

Lone--li-ness of mys--ter-y; lone--li-ness of mys-ter-y.

Where are they going when they come so quickly through the streets? Where do they sleep, and if they cannot sleep, what goes on then before their sad eyes? What do they think about when they sit all day long in the open gardens, their heads sunk over their hands which have come together as from afar, each to hide itself in the other? And what kind of words do they say to themselves when their lips summon up their strength and work? Do they still weave real words? . . . Are those still sentences they say, or is everything already crowding out of them pell-mell as out of a burning theater, everything that was spectator in them and actor, audience and hero? Does no one think of the fact that there is a childhood in them that is being lost, a strength that is sickening, a love that is falling?

O Lord, I was so tormented day after day. For I understood all those people, and although I went around them in a wide arc, they had no secret from me. I was torn out of myself into their lives, right through all their lives, through all their burdened lives. I often had to say aloud to myself that I was not one of them, that I would go away again from that horrible city in which they will die; I said it to myself and felt that it was no deception. And yet, when I noticed how my clothes were becoming worse and heavier from week to week, and saw how they were slit in many places, I was frightened and felt that I would belong irretrievably to the lost if some passer-by merely looked at me and half unconsciously counted me with them. Anyone could push me down to them with the cursory judgment of a disparaging glance. And wasn't I really one of them, since I was poor like them and full of opposition to everything that occupied and rejoiced and deluded and deceived other people? Was I not denying everything that was valid about me—and was I not actually homeless in spite of the semblance of a room in which I was as much a stranger as if I were sharing it with someone unknown? Did I not starve, like them, at tables on which stood food that I did not touch because it was not pure and not simple like that which I loved? And did I not already differ, like them, from the majority about me by the fact that no wine was in me nor any other deluding drink? Was I not clear like those lonely ones who were misted over only on the outside by the fumes and heaviness of the city and the laughter that comes like smoke out of the evil fires that it keeps going? Nothing was so little laughter as the laughter of those estranged creatures: when they laughed, it sounded as though something were falling in them, falling and being dashed to pieces and filling them up with broken bits. They were serious; and their seriousness reached out for me like the force of gravity and drew me deep down into the center of their misery. (110-112)

* * *

REFLECTION

A friend of mine, recalling an experience of getting off a train in a large metropolitan area (first time away from home), asked whether or not I thought it possible to die from loneliness. Intuitively, I answered yes. Away from the security of home and familiarity of friends and culture, it is possible to die deep within.

Another friend, of a radically different personality type, claimed never to have experienced loneliness. He made this statement in the presence of myself and two other traveling companions. The ensuing argument was intense and heated. Three against one maintained that loneliness is universal and exempts no one from its anguish. The person, devoided of contact with the "lonelys," held his claim to this exemption.

My own heart opts for the possibility of dying of loneliness as well as the claim that loneliness is universal. Semantics may well be a part of the problem here but everyone knows what it means to be cut off or abandoned, forgotten or neglected. We also know that regardless of close and intimate friends, we have a separate existence and private interior spaces that no one has access to. In some form or other, loneliness is the consequent feeling.

Mystery is necessarily lonely because of its profundity, not its incomprehensibility. Nothing is more meaningful than mystery in its essence, but because of our finite minds and constricted hearts, mystery throws us into the land of loneliness. Standing on the ocean shore, even surrounded by friends, draws us deep into the darkness of not knowing infinity; gazing at the horizon from a mountain peak plunges our imaginations into the experience of immensity; contemplating the fingers of a newborn child or pondering the death of a life-time friend—the mysteries of life and death—drives us into an inarticulateness. Mystery means not to know and that space is lonely. No one can enter into the uniqueness of our experience even though blessed with compassion. All of us stutter and stumble in the presence of a sunset, a friendship, a star. Such is life.

Something within the human spirit does not relish the land of loneliness. Yet it is a secret territory in which knowledge is discovered and life is experienced in a unique way. Too much companionship (even intimacy?) covers over the rawness of reality and prevents us from encountering the mystery of God. A note of warning must be given: the land of loneliness is especially dangerous when people lack a sense of self-worth—in such seasons loneliness leans toward suicide. When this is not the case and one has a healthy sense of one's own dignity, loneliness becomes the gateway for a life of mature spiritual quality.

Yes, it is possible to die of loneliness. The paradox is that we cannot live without it either. Yes, I suppose that some personality types never experience loneliness. My only reaction is one of pity: so much of human experience is simply foregone. Sometimes I think that loneliness resembles C. S. Lewis' land of Narnia, that land where for the first time we see and hear what truly is. To remain beyond its borders, to be caught up in the roar of the madding crowd, is the ultimate mistake. Such escapism throws us into a destructive isolation (which some unfortunately and inaccurately call loneliness) synonymous with hell. True loneliness, ultimately connecting us with the Creator and all creation, leads us into the experience of heaven.

* * *

COMMENTARY

HOMELESSNESS OF THINGS

No place to call one's own, to call one's home. No possession of those things that provide basic physical security: a roof, a bed, a chair, a table, a wardrobe. Thus some type of a loan is requested and we accept the coin or cloth from those who have. Though perhaps difficult to accept, we humans learn to bear this type of homelessness. Such a condition can be defined by means of economic analysis and careful inventory. Strange to say, homelessness at this level causes less aloneness than that experienced by those with many beds and chairs, many dwellings and abundant wines. Economic homelessness sometimes creates inner space and frees physical energy that promotes human bonding. Yet radical destitution—tragic homelessness—is destructive and paves the way for a life of bitterness and resentment. In all of this we are still far from the land of mystery. While appreciating the necessity of things and the rich delight that they provide, things do destroy or cover up the richness of life when possessed beyond moderation. Satiation deadens the spirit, extravagant possessions tax our energies, consumerism becomes a way of life—always having more and more and more. Homelessness of things is not only possible to bear but becomes necessary for an authentic spiritual life. Self-denial and asceticism have always been conditions for living the life of the spirit.

HOMELESSNESS OF HEART

A more severe homelessness, yet still somewhat definable, is that of the heart. To have no home at this level is to be a stranger to love. Not that efforts have not been made or vast energies expended in pursuit of this blessing. Yet the door leading to another's inner sanctum remains closed. Worse, a rejecting voice locks us in the outer silence. Then we reenter that obscure dwelling of inner darkness to hide.

Can this homelessness be endured? It can be and has been. The pain of human loneliness is intense and yet some meaningful tasks or social functions provide enough meaning to somewhat counterbalance the darkness within. There may even be moments of intimacy but they lack the consistency to be labeled friendship. Exiles of love, such people forage just beyond the boundaries of the promised land. Those who are not strangers to love perhaps do not touch their own obscurity. Blessed with warm relationships, they apparently experience no homelessness of heart. This is illusory. Even for those in the most tender and sacred of relationships, there is a level of existence that even our human loves cannot penetrate. This is awakened when a beloved dies, when one's own poverty is uncovered, when the silence of the night tells of the human condition. Even the "lover" knows of homelessness of heart. Their seasons may be shorter than others but the cycle cannot be stopped.

HOMELESSNESS OF THE SOUL

The land of the indefinable—the land of the soul—the country of mystery. Metaphors attempt to say something: an inexplicable and unknown leaf, a brief wind blown. Nature attempts to reveal something about the darkness of human existence. Then the painter and musician, the literary giant and sculptor give it a try but the mystery does not yield to their keys either. The grief borne here is immeasurable. Why is mystery so lonely? Why can it not be shared in all its power and agony? Our finite minds and hearts falter before its immensity. Time and space confront a foreign land. We sit on our small planet and are able to count but a few stars. Loneliness is mystery because our fingers lack sufficient strength and tenderness to hold grace.

And so *the* fact is one of exile. Our physical homes and our human loves tempt and attempt to make us deny larger realities because we cannot control or ultimately possess them. Then autumn comes with its falling leaves; then the March wind stirs and something passes through our spirits. We are reminded again and again of mystery's reality. More, the soul tastes the firmness of time and contemplates that "unimaginable tree," homelessness of the soul in the body sown.

THE MYSTIC'S PAIN

The mystic lives in light and darkness. Straddling these worlds causes intense pain. Experiencing the glory of God and then suddenly plummeted back into one's finite humanity shocks the soul's sensitivity. Mystics are not alone in this pain. All creatures, dwelling in finitude, are constantly exposed to the eternal and infinite. How does one begin to weave words around such experiences that in and of themselves are incomprehensible? Maybe it is easier to be a prophet than a mystic. At least one can do something and seem to have some control in matters of history and culture. One makes things happen instead of just letting things happen. By contrast, the mystic is given a vocation which contains noons of light and nights of darkness. In prayer the mystic ventures into this turbulent terrain and pays the price of self-denial. Homelessness! But then there was someone who once said: "Do not let your hearts be troubled." This mystic went on to speak of his Father's dwelling that had many rooms and mansions. Our homelessness can be endured because of that promise and hope. We have a home, a home reached after we have embraced the loneliness of mystery.

Radiance

MANTRA: **radiance from the angels**

SOURCE: Jessica Powers' "Ministering Spirits"

Never go anywhere without the angels
who watch God's face and listen to be sought.
Greater than you, yet they have joy to serve you.
Never go blundering through the jungle, thought,
without a clear-eyed one to part the branches,
shout snake or swamp-hole, cry a rock beware.
The angels of the Lord encamp around you
in any place you pitch your tents for prayer.

Know that your soul takes radiance from the angels.
She glories in these creatures of her kind
and sees herself thus lightsome, free as wind.
She stands abashed when the flesh rudely brings
its homage to these pure intelligences
and tries to crowd their beauty into bodies
and weight their grace with gravity of wings.[17]

* * *

PARALLEL REFERENCES

"See, I am sending an angel before you, to guard you on the way and bring you to the place I have prepared. Be attentive to him and heed his voice. Do not rebel against him, for he will not forgive your sin. My authority resides in him. If you heed his voice and carry out all I tell you, I will be an enemy to your enemies and a foe to your foes." (Exodus 23, 20-22)

"See that you never despise one of these little ones. I assure you, their angels in heaven constantly behold my heavenly Father's face." (Matthew 18, 10)

* * *

MINISTERING ANGELS
    radiance from the angels,
    radiance from the angels,

        —vigilant to the divine countenance
        —obedient to God's slightest whisper
        —cleared-eyed in the midst of earthly fog
        —campers on holy ground
        —creatures of tender glory

* * *

    radiance from the angels,
    radiance from the angels,

        —making lightsome our heavy spirits
        —cleansing our rude flesh of all impurities
        —parting jungle branches and reddish seas
        —illuminating every dark cancerous cell
        —serving with jubilant joy our slightest need

* * *

    radiance from the angels,
    radiance from the angels,

        —beauty transforming all darkness
        —grace banishing all sin
        —glory manifesting God's love
        —truth dispelling all ignorance
        —freedom transcending all gravity

* * *

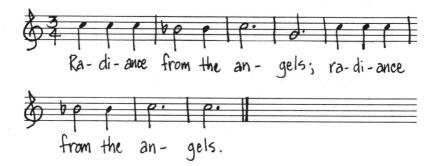

Ra- di- ance from the an- gels; ra-di-ance

from the an- gels.

radiance from the angels

PRAYER

God of angels and all nations,
source of all light and beauty,
continue to give us your protection
and the guidance of your love.
On our life's journey we face the snake's temptation,
the swamp's morass, the jungle's confusion.
Send forth your angeled truth and strength so that
we might be lightsome and transparent.
May the radiance of your angels enlighten our way. Amen.

* * *

QUOTATIONS FROM THOMAS MERTON[18]

Another focus of ambiguity: monastic world denial is originally a denial of a world that has not been penetrated with light of the Resurrection, in order to see the world that *has* been transfigured and illuminated. (644)

* * *

The reality that is present to us and in us: call it Being, call it Atman, call it Pneuma. . . or Silence. And the simple fact that by being attentive, by learning to listen (or recovering the natural capacity to listen which cannot be learned any more than breathing), we can find ourself engulfed in such happiness that it cannot be explained: the happiness of being at one with everything in that hidden ground of Love for which there can be no explanations. (115)

* * *

But indeed we exist solely for this, to be the place He has chosen for His presence, His manifestation in the world, His epiphany. But we make all this dark and inglorious because we fail to believe it, we refuse to believe it. It is not that we hate God, rather we hate ourselves, despair of ourselves: if we once began to recognize, humbly but truly, the real value of our own self, we would see that this value was the sign of God in our being, the signature of God upon our being. Fortunately, the love of our fellow man is given us as the way of realizing this. For the love of our brother, our sister, our beloved, our wife, our child, is there to see with the clarity of God Himself that we are good. It is the love of my lover, my brothers or my child that sees God in me, make God credible to myself in me. And it is my love for my lover, my child, my brother, that enables me to show God to him or her in himself or herself. Love is the epiphany of God in our poverty. (157)

* * *

I believe my vocation is essentially that of a pilgrim and an exile in life, that I have no proper place in this world but that for that reason I am in some sense to be the friend and brother of people everywhere, especially those who are exiles and pilgrims like myself. . . My life is in many ways simple, but it is also a mystery which I do not attempt to really understand, as though I were led by the hand in a night where I see nothing, but can fully depend on the Love and Protection of Him Who guides me. (52)

* * *

REFLECTION

In the face of mystery, laughter is sometimes the only resort. Philosophers have tried to construct and explain "the chain of being," ranging from inanimate matter to the notion of being as being (*ens qua ens*). In attempting to insert some type of being between God (infinite, spiritual being) and the human person (that strange composite of matter and spirit), angels have fit the category. Lacking flesh yet not divine, the angels are pure spirits and, stumbling to explain their essence, the agnostic philosopher/theologian questions the number of angels that might be able to get on a rather small dance floor: the head of a pin.

So a poet enters and rather than raise theoretical questions makes some assertions: angels watch God's face in loving obedience; angels desire to be in the service of God's designs; angels wait upon us "not so great" human beings (and the angels do this with joy); angels part the branches of our confusion and warn us of dangers; angels come around every time we raise our minds and hearts to God; angels give radiance to the soul and on and on and on. Is this all a phantasy or are we in the heartland of faith? The marvelous ballet "The Nutcracker" gives us small, childlike angels with wings of no small power. Our image of angels often comes from such sources and the "drawings" of scriptures. But God's angels are more substantive than these. Whenever truth crosses our path, whenever love touches our heart, whenever justice is promoted or protected, whenever freedom is won anew, be assured that some angel of God has just passed through. Perhaps our eyes are too slow to hear and our hearts too hard to feel, but an angel was there. The after-effects of lightsomeness, courage, transparency provided evidence, not of some exotic dance on the head of a pin, but of the burning sword of God's presence that makes us into loving and caring individuals. Philosophers have a duty to search out wisdom just as theologians have the obligation to explain our faith as coherently as possible. Better that they do these tasks than conjecture about dancing angels.

* * *

COMMENTARY

What do angels do? Do they have a "position description" that not only gives us a lead as to their tasks but also hints at their very identity? How about the following?

a) watch God's face	(worship and praise)
b) listen to be sought	(obedient availability)
c) part the branches	(guidance))
d) shout and cry warnings	(protection)
e) encamp around humans	(presence)
f) offer radiance	(offer light and glory)
g) lightsome, free as wind	(transcend time & space)
h) pure intelligences	(knowledgeable)
i) beauty	(gracious because graced)

As a pilgrim people, it is possible that we dare to travel alone. Our self-sufficiency and independence tempt us to neglect the support and assistance of both human and divine help. Thus the poet's imperative: "Never go anywhere without the angels." Our mind easily gets confused in the jungle of pluralistic thought. Our daily decisions confront swamp-holes, stumbling blocks and rocks as well as Genesis' ubiquitous serpent. Even when we, however feebly, lift our minds and hearts to God in prayer, our tents are surrounded by messengers delivering and transmitting communications. To travel alone is perhaps the most foolish of all human endeavors.

Something deep within the recesses of our enfleshed beings identifies with angelic creatures. Indeed, our deepest self is of the same species: lightsome, intelligent, filled with loving beauty. When placed near the sun, the crystal takes on a brilliant radiance. When near the angels, our souls are filled with light and transparency. Yet something obstructs the radiance from doing its work. Our flesh finds the light foreign and yearns again for darkness and the weight of earth. Certain altitudes make breathing difficult and inspire spiritual vertigo. Better the cave, says the body, than the mountain peaks.

Grace and beauty mark angelic existence. Grace and beauty also mark the human journey on occasion, just as sin and ugliness stain our travels. With precise intentionality our souls can, says a poet, "select her own society." With whom shall we travel: alone, with another human being, with the angels? Well advised is the winter traveler to have a full tank of gas and warm clothing along. The winter is long, the darkness is deep. Well advised is the human pilgrim to travel with the angels who, though "greater than you, yet have joy to serve you." Angels lead us into springtime, into grace and beauty. Soon the winter will be over and the darkness vanished. Till then, select noble companions for the soul's society.

Mystery

MANTRA: **the vigil of mystery**

SOURCE: Jessica Powers' "To Live with the Spirit"

To live with the Spirit of God is to be a listener.
It is to keep the vigil of mystery,
earthless and still.
One leans to catch the stirring of the Spirit,
strange as the wind's will.

The soul that walks where the wind of the Spirit blows
turns like a wandering weather-vane toward love.
It may lament like Job or Jeremiah,
echo the wounded hart, tho matcless dove.
It may rejoice in spaciousness of meadow
that emulates the freedom of the sky.
Always it walks in waylessness, unknowing;
it has cast down forever from its hand
the compass of the whither and the why.

To live with the Spirit of God is to be a lover.
It is becoming love, and like to Him
toward Whom we strain with metaphors of creatures:
fire-sweep and water-rush and the wind's whim.
The soul is all activity, all silence;
and though it surges Godward to its goal,
it holds, as moving earth holds sleeping noonday,
the peace that is the listening of the soul. [19]

* * *

71

PARALLEL REFERENCES

> My soul yearns for you in the night,
>   yes, my spirit within me keeps vigil for you;
> When your judgment dawns upon the earth,
>   the world's inhabitants learn justice.
> The wicked man, spared, does not learn justice:
>   in an upright land he acts perversely,
>   and sees not the majesty of the Lord. (Isaiah 26, 9-10)

* * *

> I was sleeping, but my heart kept vigil;
>   I heard my lover knocking:
> "Open to me, my sister, my beloved,
>   my dove, my perfect one!
> For my head is wet with dew,
>   my locks with the moisture of the night."
> I have taken off my robe,
>   am I then to put it on?
> I have bathed my feet,
>   am I then to soil them?
> My lover put his hand through the opening;
>   my heart trembled within me,
>   and I grew faint when he spoke.
> I rose to open to my lover,
>   with hands dripping myrrh:
> With fingers dripping choice myrrh
>   upon the fittings of the lock.
> I opened to my lover—
>   but my lover had departed, gone.
> I sought him but I did not find him;
>   I called to him but he did not answer me.
> (Songs of Songs 5, 2-6)

* * *

THE VIGIL OF MYSTERY

the vigil of mystery,
the vigil of mystery

the mystery of the star—wandering lost in a distant galaxy
the mystery of a flame—chasing away night's fearful deed
the mystery of a flower—teaching soft beauty to the heart
the mystery of a word—unveiling the secrets of hidden thought
the mystery of a tear—disclosing the moisture of compassion

the vigil of mystery
the vigil of mystery

the mystery of a stone—enduring the harshness of winter
the mystery of a lark—welcoming the golden dawn
the mystery of a hug—embracing years of care
the mystery of a glance—bonding lovers across the room
the mystery of a welcome—ending the exile of loneliness

the vigil of mystery
the vigil of mystery

the mystery of a dance—throwing one's soul into ecstasy
the mystery of a mountain—measuring the vastness of God
the mystery of a friend—forging a union of mind and heart
the mystery of a diamond—concealing a prism of deep purples
the mystery of a dawn—birthing a glorious, new day

the vigil of mystery
the vigil of mystery

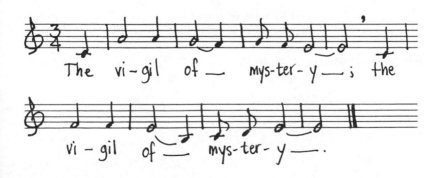

PRAYER

God of mystery and silence, help us to sit at your feet and contemplate the marvels that surround us. May we watch with eager longing for the intrusions of grace; may we rejoice in the splendor of your beauty. Listeners and lovers we are to become through the power of your grace. Help our souls to walk where your Spirit blows.

* * *

QUOTES FROM SIMONE WEIL [20]

For us, this obedience of things in relation to God is what the transparency of a window pane is in relation to light. As soon as we feel this obedience with our whole being, we see God. (xxii)

* * *

The whole space is filled, even though sounds can be heard, with a dense silence which is not an absence of sound but is a positive object of sensation; it is the secret world, the world of Love who holds us in his arms from the beginning. (87)

* * *

Only by the supernatural working of grace can a soul pass through its own annihilation to the place where alone it can get the sort of attention which can attend to truth and to affliction. It is the same attention which listens to both of them. The name of this intense, pure, disinterested, gratuitous, generous attention is love. (333)

* * *

Humility is a certain relation of the soul to time. It is an acceptance of waiting. That is why, socially, it is the mark of inferiors that they are made to wait. "I nearly had to wait" is the tyrant's word. But in ceremony, whose poetry makes all men equal, everybody has to wait. (424)

* * *

That is a turning away of our eyes, for love is the soul's looking. It means that we have stopped for an instant to wait and to listen. (489)

* * *

REFLECTION

Often in the early hours of winter mornings I have sat, wrapped in darkness, gazing into the flame of a candle. The flame, like myself, was fragile, too easily snuffed out. The flame was enchanting, fleeting, quixotic in its morning dance. The flame was all mystery in its origin and destiny.

Scientists surely could describe its chemical components and combustive dynamics. For scientists and their like hold desperately to the compass of the whither and the why. But as to having instruments to measure the qualities of the flame's listener and lover, here they falter. No technology has access to the mystery of a flame or a human person.

The candle and its small brilllance are symbolic of so many daily mysteries that circle around each of us: the mystery of dialogue and memory, the mystery of a bird's flight and human metabolism, the mystery of a new hope or an old love. Lacking the ability to comprehend fully any of these, we are well advised to assume the role of listener and lover.

The ways of knowing are many. Aggressively we reach in to dissect the truth and in our bold analyses destroy the very thing we seek to possess. With some degree of ambiguity we seek to know the thoughts of friends through conversation or shared affection. Humbly we enter the land of mystery where we, no longer active and controlling, submit to the reality that now possesses us. Mystery happens only at these receptive moments—a gracious surrender of ourselves to Another.

Though mystery is ever present, it is too seldom experienced. The flame burns but our hearts are insensitive or preoccupied. The dawn comes but we are asleep. The hawk soars but our eyes are cast down. The stars illumine the dark heavens but the city lights obscure their brilliance.

A new/ancient virtue must be planted and nurtured. It is the seed of waiting, of watching, of vigilance. This disposition is hard won in an environment hostile to enigma and obsessed with clarity. Mystery tends to hide, like a shy, small child, when faced with acquisitive eyes and avaricious hands. Mystery is easily seduced by those who wait and listen and love. Then it comes out of hiding in all its glory, a glory as small as a winter's candle and as vast as the summer's sun.

* * *

COMMENTARY

A LISTENER

Vigils are a rather rare phenomena in our hectic and impatient world. Our culture casts an anxious eye on all waiting. We demand immediacy and our impatience with patience characterizes our life-style. Yet a failure of vigilance is a failure of depth, a failure of wisdom, a failure to be human. Revelation does not happen apart from watching and listening; mystery in all its darkness must be befriended in the stillness of the night. What is felt in our holy vigils is the stirring of the Spirit of God. These stirrings (nudges, impulses, urges, movements, proddings, whispers) cannot be apprehended amidst noise and frenetic anxiety. Too subtle for the crass soul are these stirrings of love, these whispers of mercy and justice. Only the grace of tender faith enables us to leap into the mystery of forgiveness and love. As that grace is offered and accepted we catch the movements of our God.

Omnis comparatio claudicat (every simile limps). True, but that is no reason for discarding our creaturely metaphors. The wind is known to all of us. It is familiar in all its strange ways. The will of the wind cannot be controlled by human technology nor can the stirrings of God's Spirit. God's will, like that of the wind, blows where it wills.

A WALKER

The paths of life are many. More than two roads diverge through the yellow wood. Each of us has to make a choice as to where we will walk, what our destinations (and therefore our destinies) will be. A decision to place ourselves in the wind of love, and thus become forever a wandering weather-vane, demands courage of immense proportions. Such a choice means that we are daily, hourly, monthly, available to whatever breeze God sends. All predetermined maps and every person-ally-constructed compass are thrown away. What happens on such a chosen path? Lamentation for sure: the losses of a Job, the inadequacy of a Jeremiah, the pain of love's arrow, the loneliness of the dove. Yet love's path contains joys as well: the large spacious world of the common good, the freedoms of justice and courage, the immensity of grace. Living this life of ambiguity and ambivalence (lamentation and rejoicing) expresses our confidence in God's creation. We embrace the world and our creatureliness the way they are, unwilling to construct our own illusive utopias. Only on this road of love can we walk with God's Spirit.

This path contains an "always" and a "forever." Faith invites us into waylessness and the land of unknowing. Trust enables us to forego the assurance of a compass that attempts to secure direction and meaning. We follow the Lord on the road to Calvary and we participate in the cross of poverty. The only compass we look to are the four directional beams of incarnate and crucified love.

A LOVER

Love takes a long time to come to full bloom. The process of becoming, painful in its many seasons, is the goal of all life. When all the specific social roles are set aside there is but a single identity which qualifies us as humans: to be a lover. Grounded in the theology that God is love, we come to realize that to live in God is to live in love.

Metaphors attempt to speak of the mystery of God's Spirit, the Spirit of love. Love is fire that sweeps through the mountains and valleys of creation, igniting all in glorious consummation. Love is water rushing down the gorges of time with beauty and power and transparency. Love is the wind whose whim no finite human heart can embrace. In all these figures there is both activity and silence, movement and stillness. The Spirit of God causes love to spread down the crevices of time.

The ultimate sign of life in the Spirit is peace. This grace flows from union with God and unity among ourselves. Though always piecemeal on this human journey, peace is a reality that comes when the soul listens and responds with love. Obedience it is that puts our homes and community, our nations and fragile planet at rest. Obedience gives us peace.

Advent

MANTRA: **I wait in Mary-Darkness / hidden in this dark with me**

SOURCE: Jessica Powers' "Advent"

> I live my Advent in the womb of Mary.
> And on one night when a great star swings free
> from its high mooring and walks down the sky
> to be the dot above the *Christus i,*
> I shall be born of her by blessed grace.
> I wait in Mary-darkness, faith's walled place,
> with hope's expectance of nativity.
>
> I knew for long she carried me and fed me,
> guarded and loved me, though I could not see.
> But only now, with inward jubilee,
> I come upon earth's most amazing knowledge:
> *someone is hidden in this dark with me.*[21]

* * *

PARALLEL REFERENCES

Again the Lord spoke to Ahaz: Ask for a sign from the Lord, your God; let it be deep as the nether world, or high as the sky! But Ahaz answered, "I will not ask! I will not tempt the Lord!" Then he said: Listen, O house of David! Is it not enough for you to weary men, must you also weary my God? Therefore the Lord himself will give you this sign: the virgin shall be with child, and bear a son, and shall name him Immanuel. He shall be living on curds and honey by the time he learns to reject the bad and choose the good. For before the child learns to

reject the bad and choose the good, the land of those two kings whom
you dread shall be deserted. (Is 7, 10-16)

* * *

Now this is how the birth of Jesus Christ came about. When his
mother Mary was engaged to Joseph, but before they lived together, she
was found with child through the power of the Holy Spirit. Joseph her
husband, an upright man unwilling to expose her to the law, decided to
divorce her quietly. Such was his intention when suddenly the angel of
the Lord appeared in a dream and said to him: "Joseph, son of David,
have no fear about taking Mary as your wife. It is by the Holy Spirit
that she has conceived this child. She is to have a son and you are to
name him Jesus because he will save his people from their sins. All this
happened to fulfill what the Lord had said through the prophet:

> "The virgin shall with be child
> and give birth to a son,
> and they shall call him Emmanuel,"

a name which means "God is with us." (Mt 1, 18-23)

* * *

MARY DARKNESS

> I wait in Mary-darkness,
> I wait in Mary-darkness,
>
>> for some great star to swing free,
>> for light to conquer the night,
>> for midnight sadness to turn to morning jubilee ,
>> for a hidden someone to set me free.
>
> I wait in Mary-darkness,
> I wait in Mary-darkness,
>
>> as one concerned and carried in love,
>> as one walled in faith's small place,
>> as one expectant of know-not-what,
>> as one blessed by a walking star.

I wait in Mary-darkness,
I wait in Mary-darkness,

        in wonder at the amazing knowledge of presence,
        in gratitude for being guarded so long,
        in fear of star's staying home,
        in certainty that darkness is Mary-ed and Christ-ed.

PRAYER

In the darkness of midnight we await your coming, O Lord. The silence of the angels' song, the fidelity of the shepherds' watch, the eternal dance of the stars join in this Advent moment. Bless us with the hope that every day we will discover you in the darkness of our world. Teach us the patience of Mary, the courage of Joseph.

* * *

QUOTATIONS FROM HENRY DAVID THOREAU[22]

The millions are awake enough for physical labor; but only one in a million is awake enough for effective intellectual exertion, only one in a hundred million to a poetic or divine life. To be awake is to be alive. I have never yet met a man who was quite awake. How could I have looked him in the face? (65)

* * *

The greatest gains and values are farthest from being appreciated. We easily come to doubt if they exist. We soon forget them. They are the highest reality. Perhaps the facts most astounding and most real are never communicated by man to man. The true harvest of my daily life is somewhat as intangible and indescribable as the tints of morning or evening. It is a little star-dust caught, a segment of the rainbow which I have clutched. (147)

I wait in Mar-y dark-ness; I
wait in Mar-y dark - ness.

Simplicity, simplicity, simplicity! I say, let your affairs be as two or three, and not a hundred or a thousand; instead of a million count half a dozen, and keep your account on your thumb-nail. . . . Simplify, simplify. Instead of three meals a day, if it be necessary eat but one; instead of a hundred dishes, five; and reduce other things in proportion. (66)

* * *

I find it wholesome to be alone the greater part of the time. To be in company, even with the best, is soon wearisome and dissipating. I love to be alone. (95)

* * *

But the notes of the flute came home to his ears out of a different sphere from that he worked in, and suggested work for certain faculties which slumbered in him. (151)

REFLECTION

My father was a medical doctor who served our small rural village of Boar Creek, Wisconsin, from 1933 until 1970. Surgery, counseling, dispensing of medication filled his days. What often filled his nights was the delivery of a baby. Once I was with him on such an occasion and watched as baby left the warmth and darkness of womb to burst forth into our cold and glaring world.

Each of us spends nine months in our mother's womb where we are carried and fed, hopefully, guarded and loved. Yet something deep in our fetal hearts longs for nativity.

At birth, we leave the loneliness of our mother's womb to be plunged into the womb of the earth, God's larger creation. Here we are carried by the air, fed by the wheat field, guarded by law and constitutions, loved by friends. In faith, we realize God's hidden presence at every juncture of our lives. The Mystical Body assures us that we are not alone but await our eternal nativity with all of humankind. If, at times, our hope weakens, ever so often our heart stirs, like a February oak tree, with the quickening of spring.

But faith knowledge is rare these days. "Earth's most amazing knowledge" is learned by few. The forces of individualism and greed, the hurried lifestyle that keeps us in hummingbird flight, the explosion of knowledge and the complexity of our universe—all of these militate against our resting in and living with an awareness that "someone is hidden in this dark with me."

At times we do not have options regarding where we live. Finances or employment circumstances dictate that we live in Chicago and not Phoenix, Tampa and not Seattle. But no circumstance need keep us from selecting our own inner society, our own interior geography. We can decide that our Advent and our entire lives will be lived in "faith's walled place," in the womb of Mary. We can, with intention and full deliberation, choose to dwell in the darkness with Christ.

The delivery of a baby is a somewhat violent moment. Even more violent is going back into the womb of faith from our secular lifestyle. Indeed, it demands a dying to self. By that very deed we are united with him who died for all on the cross.

* * *

COMMENTARY

Lord, I have chosen to live in such diverse places: the land of self-indulgence, the field of pleasure and pain, the meadow of work, the mountains of fear, the valley of despair. Too varied has my geography been and too often lost in foolish wanderings. But now, if your mercy permits, for a space of time I live within the wombed wall of your loving mother, Mary. Only your grace allows me to choose freely this darkness where burns the greatest lantern of all; only your providential love enables me to leave behind the false lights of things and activities so as to enter your presence; only your gracious mercy can purify me and strip me of all that is incompatible with your dwelling.

Nicodemus struggled with the mystery of rebirth. So do I, Lord. How to be reborn, how to re-enter the sacred space of your grace, how to be reshaped at the potter's wheel when the clay has been hardened for many decades. So powerful is your love that all obstacles fall away as you draw us once again into the matrix of your creative touch. Help me to die to every stirring that draws me away from you. Grace all of us, every day, to be reborn anew with the rising of the sun. May we be the dot above the *Christus i.*

Waiting is such a painful process. Not to have, not to hold, to sit empty and alone—waiting, waiting, waiting. Lord, grant us two graces throughout the course of our lives until we are born fully into your kingdom: the grace of faith and the grace of hope. In this walled place of planet earth, in this walled place of our faith in your Mystical Body, we do not see clearly. We live in trustful adherence to your promise and know, deep down in the crevices of our being, that you are near and that you care. We live with expectancy that one day we will experience full nativity. Some day, some century, some eternity, our half-truths and half-loves must yield to fullness of being. Meanwhile, in faith and in hope we wait in Mary-darkness.

Certitude is not abundant in our times. Relativity, agnosticism, doubt, ignorance stalk our land and conquer many minds and hearts. But there is one thing I know, whether it comes from faith or reason, who knows? I know that I have been carried, fed, guarded and loved. In my heart of hearts, there is a certitude so deep that no darkness can take it away. Intuition, not sight, tells me of this reality. And for this I rejoice and am filled with a quiet jubilee. I do not sing aloud lest the noise distort the silent music of your nearness.

Lord, you have added to this knowledge of being wombed in Mary yet another grace. We dwell not alone in Mary-darkness. We wait not alone in faith and love. We are carried and loved not simply as individuals but as a people. For you have come into our darkness, O Emmanuel, and abide with us. Hidden though you are, you make your presence felt in every quickening, arising from epiphanies of truth and love and justice. Hidden though you be, you are manifest in the cry of the poor, the hunger of the afflicted, the loneliness of the refugee. So unhidden are you, at times, that we see you in every sister and brother who intersects our lives with some grace or need. So large is the womb of Mary that all creation can be found there.

Lord, may we always live in faith and hope, we may always live in the womb of Mary. More, may we live in love and reach out to you in others whenever and wherever you call us to be instruments of your peace. Amazing knowledge indeed: "Someone is hidden in this dark with me."

Eternity

MANTRA: **native to eternity**

SOURCE: Jessica Powers' "The Homecoming"

The spirit, newly freed from earth,
is all amazed at the surprise
of her belonging: suddenly
as native to eternity
to see herself, to realize
the heritage that lets her be
at home where all this glory lies.

By naught foretold could she have guessed
such welcome home: the robe, the ring,
music and endless banqueting,
these people hers; this place of rest
known, as of long remembering
herself a child of God and pressed
with warm endearments to His breast.[23]

* * *

PARALLEL REFERENCES

While he [the prodigal son] was still a long way off, his father caught sight of him and was deeply moved. He ran out to meet him, threw his arms around his neck, and kissed him. The son said to him, "Father, I have sinned against God and against you; I no longer deserve to be called your son." The father said to his servants: "Quick! bring out the finest robe and put it on him; put a ring on his finger and shoes on his feet. Take the fatted calf and kill it. Let us eat and celebrate because this son of mine was dead and has come back to life. He was lost and is found." Then the celebration began. (Lk 15, 20-24)

* * *

But now in Christ Jesus you who once were far off have been brought near through the blood of Christ. It is he who is our peace, and who made the two of us one by breaking down the barrier of hostility that kept us apart. In his own flesh he abolished the law with its command and precepts, to create in himself one new man for us who had been two and to make peace, reconciling both of us to God in one body through his cross, which put that enmity to death. He came and "announced the good news of peace to you who were far off, and to those who were near"; through him we both have access in one Spirit to the Father. This means that you are strangers and aliens no longer. No, you are fellow citizens of the saints and members of the household of God. (Eph 2, 13-19)

* * *

NATIVE TO ETERNITY
        native to eternity
        native to eternity

                —passing through death's door
                the angels acclaim the return of the native

                —on the other side of the door:
                        wild meadows
                        vast skies
                        rainbow upon rainbow of colors
                        water pure and refreshing
                        the embrace of peace

                —newly freed from earth
                time is foreign and eternity the only reality

        native to eternity
        native to eternity

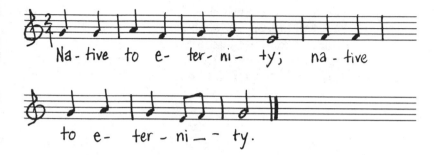

Na-tive to e- ter-ni- ty; na - tive

to e- ter - ni ___ - ty.

PRAYER

God of time and eternity,
Lord of heaven and earth,
may we hear upon the stillness of death
the whisper of "Beloved," the good news
of "well done." More, may we see
your face of mercy and feel the touch of your tenderness.
Call us home, we who are native to eternity, that we
may find in you our true country and the mystery of peace.

* * *

QUOTATIONS FROM ST. BERNARD OF CLAIRVAUX[24]

For our deeds do not pass away as they seem to. On the contrary, every deed done in this life is the seed of a harvest to be reaped in eternity. (79)

* * *

What is the result of contemplating such great mercy and mercy so undeserved, such generous and proven love, such unlooked-for condescension, such persistent gentleness, such astonishing sweetness? To what, I ask, will all these wonderfully draw and deeply attract the thoughtful mind when it considers them carefully and is wholly set at liberty from unworthy love? It will despise everything else, everything which will get in the way of that desire. (184)

Are you wondering how she was able to change like this, or how she deserved it? You shall hear in a few words. She wept bitterly (Lk 22, 62) and sighed deeply from her inmost heart, and her sobs shook her one by one, and the evils within her came forth. The heavenly Physician came quickly to help her, for "his Word runs swiftly" (Ps 147, 15). (221)

* * *

What, then, is God? He is the purpose to which the universe looks, the salvation of the elect. What he is to himself, only he knows. What is God? All-powerful will, benevolent virtue, eternal light, changeless reason, supreme blessedness. He creates minds to share in himself, gives them life, so that they may experience him, causes them to desire him, enlarges them to grasp him, justifies them so that they may deserve him, stirs them to zeal, ripens them to fruition, directs them to equity, forms them in benevolence, moderates them to make them wise, strengthens them to virtue, visits them to console, enlightens them with knowledge, sustains them to immortality, fills them with happiness, surrounds them with safety. (166)

* * *

You must look for higher goods in the higher part of yourself, that is, the soul. These higher goods are dignity, knowledge, virtue. Man's dignity is his free will, which is the gift by which he is superior to the animals and even rules them (Gen 1, 26). Man's knowledge is that by which he recognizes that he possesses this dignity, but that it does not originate in himself. His virtue is that by which he seeks eagerly for his Creator, and when he finds him, holds to him with all his might. (176)

* * *

To love in this way is to become like God. As a drop of water seems to disappear completely in a quantity of wine, taking the wine's flavor and color; as red-hot iron becomes indistinguishable from the glow of fire and its own original form disappears; as air suffused with the light of the sun seems transformed into the brightness of the light, as if it

were itself light rather than merely lit up; so, in those who are holy, it
is necessary for human affection to dissolve in some ineffable way, and
be poured into the will of God. How will God be all in all (1 Cor 15:26)
if anything of man remains in man? The substance remains, but in another form, with another glory, another power. (196)

* * *

REFLECTION

In the autumn of 1973 I read the seven volumes of C.S. Lewis'
Chronicles of Narnia. Again in 1990, I reread the fairy tales in prepara-
tion for a summer school course on this great Anglican writer. The

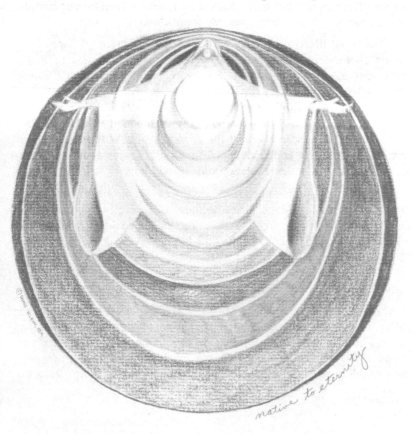

native to eternity

stories of Narnia are about good and evil, witches and queens, adventure and betrayal. A consistent question emerges: what is reality and where is our true country? More directly: are we native to eternity or time, people of immortality or mere mortals, citizens of Aslan's country or residents forever on this side of the wardrobe?

Lewis' underlying theology is clear: God is the only Reality and all other reality is derivative. Human persons are immortal and of infinite worth. In faith (in mere Christianity) we are native to eternity for we are destined to dwell with God, the Eternal One. The decisive point is to choose "sides": to opt for light or darkness, for love or selfishness, for fidelity and courage or idolatry and cowardice. The door of choice is ever before us and our ultimate destiny is determined by our cumulative decisions.

What is the lifestyle of those who are native to eternity? Two dispositions characterize those who experience the enchantment of divine grace: adoration and obedience. Put more simply: seeing and doing. Those who side with God joyfully bow down before the Mystery of Love. Natives to eternity are at home with reverence and wonder, awe and splendor, glory and transcendence. With subdued voices and quivering hearts, their faces manifest the *presence* of a Wisdom and Power that causes both fear and gladness. Adoration becomes a way of life for those who *believe* in the revelation of love and hope.

Those who are native to eternity are the obedient ones. According to the theologian John Macquarrie, holiness is basically obedience in a particular situation. Though we have known the exile of disobedience and the darkness of rebellion, the call home echoes down the corridor of time. As soon as we step across the threshold into the room of faithful obedience, a peace is experienced that no trauma can break. *Pax et obedientia:* the path to peace is along the road of obedience.

Thomas Hardy's novel *The Return of the Native* tells the tale of the native's return to Egdon Heath. It is a human story of comings and goings, often a return from one exile into another. But there are moments of eternity, moments of love as well. In the center of temporality, the eternal can be felt; in the process of dying, immortality is known;

in the transitory deeds of human exchange, something perdures. The wonder of it all: to be native to eternity not only when freed from earth but in our daily living.

* * *

COMMENTARY

BELONGING

Lord, what a mystery is death, that sometimes quiet, sometimes violent passage from time into eternity. We flounder and reel before its darkness, stumbling and trembling as we watch friends and strangers pass through this final portal.

Those who die leave behind all that is familiar: old sweaters and worn shoes, titles to home and deeds to hard-earned property, beloved seasons and family pets. Those many things that gave a sense of "at homeness" and "belonging" are stripped away; naked, we return to our origin. Newly-freed (some would think newly-deprived) from such familiarity, how does the soul respond to what awaits it in eternity? Faith holds that we have moved from realities to Reality, from shadows into the light, from half-truths and divided loves into fullness of being *(pleroma)*.

Amazement floods our souls; surprise overwhelms our narrow misconceptions and peals away our idolatries. While thinking we had lost our homes and friends and precious possessions, we discover, for the first time, alas, that we were dwelling in exile and have only now come to our native land. Here, in eternity, nothing is lost: no cup of cold water given to the thirsty, no beauty of a rainbow or sunset that pierced the human heart, no word of truth spoken whatever the cost. Through the portal of death all that was truth and good and beautiful follows us and we are imbued with their full glory. Here we belong because here is fullness of Life.

GLORY

Gracious God, because of our weakness and sin, we spend countless hours in the alleys of dead-end streets, in the deep, dark valleys of doubt and despair. We have opted, not for glory and light, but for darkness and chaos. Following the old Adam, deceived by the apple's false appearance, we have tasted of evil and sought power apart from you. We have freely chosen to walk away from glory and the splendor of your face into the nothingness of sin.

But now, in your providential mercy, you reclaim us through the glory of the cross so that the heritage promised through Abraham might be ours. While native to time we were unable to comprehend and to embrace the mystery of your love, which, when made manifest, is glory. Our interior blindness and our half-conscious existence were immune to your extravagant and overwhelming care. We passed by the color purple time and time again; we missed the touch of your tender mercy; we were deaf to your haunting plea to return home. Now, on the other side of the door, we are given this heritage of glory as if it were a wedding ring worn for 80 years. It fits, it is a part of the index finger, it symbolizes everything.

"My paradise—the fame / that they—pronounce my name." (Emily Dickinson). It is in eternity that we are known by name, our true name: "Beloved." And to think that they, the communion of saints, would also know our name startles us. Any other fame is worthless, any other heritage should be thrown upon the fire and burned. Here, in the corridors of eternity, we watch the separation of wheat and chaff and find in the pure, golden grain the glory of God. Lord, grant us your glory, give us your heritage.

WELCOME

Backpackers, who are away from civilization for weeks on end traversing mountains and deep woods, dream about the journey's end: a warm shower, seeing old friends, and rest. Be the journey prodigal or straight, we long for divine hospitality and the warm embrace of our God's gracious love. Will the robe of forgiveness fit our shoulders? Will the ring of friendship slide over the knuckles of betrayal and infidelity? Will the discordant music that too often directs our feet away from paradise be transformed into symphonies of holiness? Will our taste buds gain a new sensitivity to things divine? Along the road these questions haunt us.

Jesus, in your story of the prodigal son you did not allow the father to express a single word of admonition. So moved was the father by the return of his own flesh and blood that his only response was joy, a joy that bursts forth in the need for celebration. What sorrow pierced his heart when the elder son failed to share his joy. What grief clouded this feast because a brother could not welcome a brother home. There is only one ultimate anxiety: the closed door.

But it is not the robe or ring, the music or endless banqueting that tells the story of divine hospitality. Rather, it is the embrace of a parent's love and the gathering at table with friends. Deep in our individual and collective unconscious we sense the mystery of this intimacy. We were made for union and unity, and homecoming brings those goals to completion. Oh, death, where is your sting? Oh, death, be not proud. Oh, death, strange brother, hide not your wisdom from us.

God's Will

MANTRA: **the beautiful will of God**

SOURCE: Jessica Powers' "The Will of God"

Time has one song alone. If you are heedful
and concentrate on sound with all your soul,
you may hear the song of the beautiful will of God,
soft notes or deep sonorous tones that roll
like thunder over time.
Not many have the hearing for this music,
and fewer still have sought it as sublime.

Listen, and tell your grief: But God is singing!
God sings through all creation with His will,
Save the negation of sin, all is His music,
even the notes that set their roots in ill
to flower in pity, pardon or sweet humbling.
Evil finds harshness of the rack and rod
in tunes where good finds tenderness and glory.

The saints who loved have died of this pure music,
and no one enters heaven till he learns,
deep in his soul at least, to sing with God.[25]

* * *

PARALLEL REFERENCES

Sing to the Lord a new song
   of praise in the assembly of the faithful.
Let Israel be glad in their maker,
   let the children of Zion rejoice in their king.

Let them praise his name in the festive dance,
   let them sing praise to him with timbrel and harp.
For the Lord loves his people,
   and he adorns the lowly with victory.
Let the faithful exult in glory;
   let them sing for joy upon their couches;
let the high praises of God be in their throats. (Ps 149, 1-6)

* * *

Yes, God so loved the world
that he gave his only Son,
that whoever believes in him may not die
but may have eternal life.
God did not send the Son into the world
to condemn the world,
but that the world might be saved through him. (Jn 3, 16-17)

* * *

GOD SINGS THROUGH ALL CREATION
   God sings through all creation
   God sings through all creation

      —soft notes
               of a purple sunset
               of a friend's embrace
               of a solitary walk
               of a tide's ebb and flow
               of a baby's delicate skin

* * *

God sings through all creation
God sings through all creation

   —deep sonorous tones
            of angels emptying the floodgates
            of judges meting out justice

of doctors telling of death
of farmers preparing for droughts
of prisoners aware of their guilt

* * *

God sings through all creation
God sings through all creation

—pure music
                    the robin's joyful songs at morn
                    the waterfall's downward crash at noon
                    the sunflower's bow to the west
                    the smile exchanged between lovers
                    the letter of loving concern

PRAYER

God of song and dance, of work and play, of laughter and grief, give us hearing—the hearing of your sublime and delicate music. In boldness we ask for even more: not merely to hear but to sing with you. Inspire our hearts to chant your love and forgiveness, to hum your freedom and justice, to intone your truth and holiness always and everywhere. May our grief join your song and may your song transform our sorrow into joy. Grant this in Jesus' name. Amen.

* * *

QUOTATIONS FROM WALTER BRUEGGEMANN[26]

The mystery of God is not a general good feeling. It is a *plan*. The world is created for a purpose. That purpose will work its way. Human persons can be part of that purpose. They can, at most, delay the plan. But they cannot resist it. That is, wisdom finally drives Israel toward the resilient, even if hidden, sovereignty of God. While the experiences of the world may be presented in many different ways, all of them attest to the one who governs this life-giving process in his own inscrutable pleasure. (82)

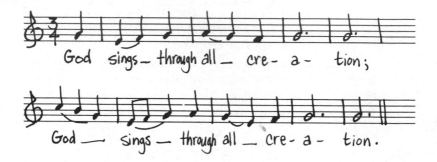

God sings — through all — cre- a - tion;

God — sings — through all — cre- a - tion.

Wisdom is to fear God, to let God be God, to let mystery be defini-
tional for life. Understanding is to depart from evil, that is, to stay at
the concrete, daily task of human community with all its ethical risks.
(89)

* * *

Communion with the God of Israel is understood primarily in terms
of *obedience*. There is no communion prior to or apart from obedience.
But obedience is the move required for communion. (101)

* * *

The best human *knowing* takes the form of *discerning obedience*.
(89)

* * *

Obedience is the primal form of biblical faith. It follows that obedience belongs to full humanness. That should not surprise us if we re-
flect on the mission of the gospel, which is to bring all creation to
joyous obedience. (101)

* * *

REFLECTION

Fiat voluntas tua!   (Thy will be done)

For two thousand years the Christian community has uttered the Lord's prayer, with reverent and thoughtless babble, with faith and creeping skepticism, with hope and blinding fear. Too seldom does the pray-er or praying community realize what is being sought. The will of God—mystery upon mystery. The divine plan understood and im-

God sings through all creation

plemented by devout disciples. Micah tells us that God's will is that we be just, love tenderly and walk in faith (6, 8). St. Paul tell us that the kingdom of God is about peace and love and joy. Romano Guardini views the kingdom as "no fixed, existing order, but a living, nearing thing." (cf. *The Lord,* p. 37)

The challenge is for every individual to discern, in unique circumstances and complex situations, what is being asked of him or her. How can one "sing with God" that divine tune that brings into existence the gift of life? Is not the key to God's will the experience of joy?

But here we must never be deceived for joy is compatible with the deepest of sufferings. God's will has something to do with oneness (its constellations involve solidarity, union, communion, unity, community). When people are bonded together in respectful, loving sharing, joy is the consequence. Be it at a wedding celebration or cancer ward, be it at harvest time or drought, be it at birth or death, joy's song lies in deep mutual sharing. God's will is that we hold hands and never let go.

This summer my brother died at age 48, leaving his wife and young children. I received the news while attending a program in California. Suddenly, outside my window I heard the shouts of children. An exuberant six-year-old girl was rounding the corner followed by her younger sister who seemed to be "fastened" to her sister's wrist by a long, elastic rope. My thoughts went over the miles to my brother's family tied to each other by their shared lives.

Now, in death, my brother was "unfastened" from his family, from me, from his friends. All we had left over were the treasured memories of what had been. But these cherished memories of family solidarity would always be with me and, in the midst of my grief, there was a moment of joy.

When deep joy stirs, the will of God is active. It is a joy that allows us to sing "soft notes or deep sonorous tones." It is a joy found even in the midst of death.

* * *

COMMENTARY

A SINGLE SONG

History has many voices: the tumult of war, the discord of racism, the cacophony of pride. Happy tunes as well: the coronation march, the melodies of compassion, the ballads of love. How can anyone, even a poet, claim that only one song courses through time? And further, that this music is "the beautiful will of God?"

But, then, perhaps the poet is right. Perhaps there is a deep listening and seeing that is not accessible to a deaf and blind culture. To speak of magenta to a blind person or to describe the cry of a whippoorwill to one who is deaf results in puzzlement. Likewise, human values find no lodging in a time-conscious world.

Yet some do recognize God's will and claim it as their way of life, even though it is a mixture of joy and pain. Faith alone reveals the beauty hidden in being in tune with the melody of God's will.

A SINGING GOD

All creation is God's song. Sunsets and rainbows, birth and death, spring rains and winter blizzards. Even the losses that break our hearts become notes in the divine symphony. We need to experience the pain, to enter into it. This is not the time for analysis, comparisons, logical reasoning. Yet, even in the darkness, the reflective Christian believes God is present and the music of his will is being written.

One thing alone finds no place in the song of creation: sin. Sin stops the music by bringing a deadly silence to all true joy. Disguised as a wild and enchanting melody, sin deceives the heart and sets the feet dancing in the direction of death.

Difficult it is for the human heart to hear God's music in trials and persecutions, sickness and disasters, pain and suffering. But from these crosses—from these apparently dead words (so resembling sin at first glance), pity, pardon and humility flower. In the end there is tenderness and glory; the rod and rack have been destroyed by Calvary's song of mercy.

SINGING WITH GOD

There is something beautiful about the solo singer or performer. The aria or cadenza (that marvelous parenthetic flourish) draws to itself the admiration of the audience, held spellbound by the melody and/or the technique of the performer. But God is not a soloist. The divine nature is in and of itself communal and thus we are invited to sing with God. What a privilege! To be co-creators, co-redeemers, co-sanctifiers with the Triune God!

Saints are singers; their song, God's will. So sublime, splendid, pure is this music that it leads to the death of self and to new life. It is the song of compassion that embraces sorrow and suffering; it is the song of obedience that is submissive to God's slightest touch; it is the melody of generosity that expresses itself in affability and graciousness.

Indwelling

in the secret of my soul

SOURCE: Jessica Powers' "In a Cloud of Angels"

> I walk in a cloud of angels.
> God has a throne in the secret of my soul.
> I move, encircled by light,
> blinded by glowing faces,
> lost and bewildered in the motion of wings,
> stricken by music too sublime to bear.
> Splendor is everywhere.
> God is always enthroned on the cherubim,
> circled by seraphim.
> Holy, holy, holy,
> wave upon wave of endless adoration.
> I walk in a cloud of angels that
> worship Him.[27]

* * *

PARALLEL REFERENCES

In the year King Uzziah died, I saw the Lord seated on a high and lofty throne, with the train of his garment filling the temple. Seraphim were stationed above; each of them had six wings: with two they veiled their faces, with two they veiled their feet, and with two they hovered aloft.

"Holy, holy, holy is the Lord of hosts!" they cried out to the other. "All the earth is filled with his glory!" At the sound of that cry, the frame of the door shook and the house was filled with smoke. (Is 6, 1-3)

When the priests left the holy place, the cloud filled the temple of the Lord so that the priests could no longer minister because of the cloud, since the Lord's glory had filled the temple of the Lord. Then Solomon said, "The Lord intends to dwell in the dark cloud; I have truly built you a princely house, a dwelling where you may abide forever." (1 Kgs 8, 10-13)

* * *

IN THE SECRET OF MY SOUL
> in the secret of my soul
> in the secret of my soul

> my soul:
>> —an empty room filled with glorious treasures
>> —a lonely island guested with a community of saints
>> —an abandoned house newly-visited by a divine stranger
>> —a barren hillside dressed in purple clover
>> —a silent mountain sung into joy

> in the secret of my soul
> in the secret of my soul

> when the angels came:
>> —a dormant seed awakening to new life
>> —a crusted field bestirred by the first furrow
>> —a black midnight set aglow with divine light
>> —an arid desert abloom with spring
>> —a wandering river come home to the sea

> in the secret of my soul
> in the secret of my soul

* * *

PRAYER

Wherever you are, Lord, in the secret of my soul, in the beauty of the autumn, in the truth of love, a cloud of angels attends your every desire. Those ministers of light hold us in the gravity of your grace. Draw us into your hidden presence that our eyes may gaze upon your

In the se-cret of my soul; in the

se-cret of my soul.

splendor, our ears hear the whispers of your silent love. Be a pillar of fire by night, a cloud of glory by day. In the secret of my soul, teach me wisdom.

QUOTATIONS FROM JEAN-PIERRE DE CAUSSADE[28]

* * *

There is a time when the soul lives in God and there is also a time
when God lives in the soul. What is appropriate to one of these conditions is inappropriate to the other. When God lives in souls, they must
surrender themselves totally to him. Whereas when souls live in God,
they must explore carefully and scrupulously every means they can find
which may lead them to their union with him. (5)

* * *

There remains one single duty. It is to keep one's gaze fixed on the
master one has chosen and to be constantly listening so as to understand and hear and immediately obey his will. (9)

* * *

It is necessary to be disengaged from all we feel and do in order to
walk with God in the duty of the present moment. All other avenues are
closed. We must confine ourselves to the present moment without taking thought for the one before or the one to come. For is not God's law
always under cover, as it were? Something will prompt us to say: "At
the moment I have a liking for this person or this book, or an inclina-
tion to take or offer this advice, to make such a complaint, to confide in
or listen to this person, or to give away this or to make that." These
stirrings of grace must be followed without relying for a single moment
on our own judgment, reason or effort. It is God who must decide what
we shall do and when, and not ourselves. When we walk with God, his
will directs us and must replace every other guidance. (15)

* * *

Since we know that divine action understands, directs and creates
everything, apart from sin, we must love and worship all it does, welcoming it with open arms. In joy and confidence we must override

everything in order to bring about the triumph of faith. That is the way to honor and acknowledge God. (22)

* * *

Did those saints of old have any secret other than to become each moment of their lives God's instruments? And will that divine action cease till the end of time to pour its grace over souls who surrender themselves totally to it? (70)

* * *

REFLECTION

The French word "ambience" refers to mood, feeling or sensibility associated with a particular person or place, thing or event. To speak of ambience is to speak of the mystery of presence and subtle atmosphere. In any given home or institution, in any group or individual contact, the most real of all things is the ambience, the environment created by the presence of the mysterious forces of personality or milieu.

Historians, poets, novelists and spiritual writers deal with ambience on a regular basis and provide us with some insights. The historian Barbara Tuchman writes: "In enclosed places such as monasteries and prisons, the infection of one person usually meant that of all" (cf. *A Distant Mirror*, 95). The philosopher-poet Ortega y Gasset states: "Tell me the landscapes in which you live and I will tell you who you are." Goethe raises the question: "Are we mere puppets of the atmosphere?" And the playwright Don Taylor reflects: "I should have let you on your farm in Oxfordshire. You were a country plant, and withered in town."

At times we have the freedom to determine the company we keep, be it amid angels or devils, frigid or tropical climates. More often we are "given" an environment not of our own making. We find ourselves walking with companions and human experiences that are thrust upon us by forces larger than the arc of our personal consciousness and self-determination. We are visited by graces: a sunset, a new friend, a meaningful insight, a compelling inspiration. Or we endure the violence of an earthquake, a cancer cell that has come to stay and grow, the termination of a job, the loss of a manuscript that held together years of research.

To walk among angels. To have God enthroned in one's soul. To experience a divine ambience that leads to light and splendor and music. Ah, to live in such a habitat where the song "holy" is the constant refrain. And to think that this atmosphere, this interior life, is available to all for the asking. To think that this is "reality" and all else is shadow-land! When will we leave the low, dark road of doubt and fear and journey in faith into the cloud of angels? There the waves of "endless adoration" plunge us into the sea of God, our true country, our true home.

* * *

COMMENTARY

The soul, graced with God's presence, is surrounded by a cloud of angels. Here there is light, splendor and sublime music. Here, in this living cathedral, there is wave upon wave of praise and thanksgiving.

How could it be otherwise? For where God is present, those creatures of light and love attend him. And to believe that all of this is happening in the secret of the human soul, that dwelling so often characterized by poverty and darkness! To think that God has built his guest room with its humble throne in the anonymous space of the human heart! Our faith deepens to hold this sublime truth. We share in Thomas' doubt when we fail to believe in angel clouds and divine thrones residing within us.

Though our lack of faith keeps us silent, God has brought along his own choir and their singing echoes down the canyons of every generation: holy, holy, holy. Those whose souls are attuned to hear this inner choir quiver with spiritual delight and joy. Cherubim and seraphim call us to loving obedience and encourage us to an ever-abiding fidelity.

Where do we walk? How do we describe our habitat and the mood of our interiority? For one poet it is to walk in a cloud of angels. This journey, filled with endless praise to the God who dwells in the soul, can be ours. Lord, increase our faith.

Humility

MANTRA: **a little feast of pleasure**

SOURCE: Jessica Powers' "Old Woman"

None walks so wise as self, so enterprising
to shift earth's precious best to her own need.
She is like some old crone that time has sharpened
to find the succulent fruit on which to feed
the wood for fuel. And she would never be
concerned that love might be a thievery.

They speak the old man in us; I find, rather,
a shrewd old woman bustling in my mind,
with woman's trickeries and subterfuges
to confiscate what her caprices find.
This is the way I make my gifts to heaven:
I follow her; I watch her and I stand
ready to wrest her treasures from her hand.
I marvel at her methods to outwit me,
her ingenuity, her self-command.
For even when I rob her utterly
she goes and makes a little feast of pleasure
out of a woe she calls humility.[29]

* * *

PARALLEL REFERENCES

Conduct your affairs with humility,
    and you will be loved more than a giver of gifts.
Humble yourself the more, the greater you are,

and you will find favor with God.
For great is the power of God;
    by the humble he is glorified.
What is too sublime for you, seek not,
    into things beyond your strength search not. (Sir 3, 17-20)

* * *

They returned to Capernaum and Jesus, once inside the house, began to ask them, "What were you discussing on the way home?" At this they fell silent, for on the way they had been arguing about who was the most important. So he sat down and called the Twelve around him and said, "If anyone wishes to rank first, he must remain the last one of all and the servant of all." Then he took a little child, stood him in their midst, and putting his arms around him, said to them, "Whoever welcomes a child such as this for my sake welcomes me. And whoever welcomes me welcomes, not me, but him who sent me." (Mk 9, 33-37)

* * *

A LITTLE FEAST OF PLEASURE
    a little feast of pleasure
    a little feast of pleasure

                —bears among blueberry bushes
                —a tree house offering rendezvous to summer children
                —salmon dancing their way north to eternity
                —a harvest moon illuminating a tawny corn field
                —a flock of asparagus discovered along a railroad track

    a little feast of pleasure
    a little feast of pleasure

                —an afternoon nap of but ten minutes
                —a spurt of water from a fourth of July hose
                —a gentle hug after weeks of affectionate drought
                —a deer, in stillness, surveying a human intrusion
                —toast and coffee on an early December morn

    a little feast of pleasure
    a little feast of pleasure

PRAYER

All good pleasure is of your making, Lord. You delight in surprising us with joy and we seek to be grateful always. Help us not to misuse your gifts of pleasure or pain; help us not to fall into the illusory joys that promise everything and give nothing. And when the days of pain come, flood our memory with your little feasts of pleasures.

a little feast of pleasure

QUOTATIONS FROM MADELEINE L'ENGLE[30]

Faith is what makes life bearable, with all its tragedies and ambiguities and sudden, startling joys. (22)

* * *

The widow's mite was worth more than all the rich men's gold because it represented the focus of her life. (31)

* * *

We cannot seem to escape paradox; I do not think I want to. (36)

* * *

We are human and humble and of the earth, and we cannot create until we acknowledge our createdness. (41)

* * *

We are suspicious of grace. We are afraid of the very lavishness of the gift. (72)

* * *

It is not easy for me to be a Christian, to believe twenty-four hours a day all that I want to believe. I stray, and then my stories pull me back if I listen to them carefully. I have often been asked if my Christianity affects my stories, and surely it is the other way around; my stories affect my Christianity, restore me, shake me by the scruff of the neck, and pull this straying sinner into an awed faith. (106)

* * *

I wasn't consciously realizing that the brain, when it is disengaged from the heart, turns vicious. (Conversely, the heart, when it is disengaged from the brain, can become sentimental and untruthful.) (172)

* * *

REFLECTION

In 1941, C.S. Lewis wrote some letters. The correspondence was unusual in that the "author" was a senior devil named Screwtape and the recipient was a younger devil, Screwtape's nephew, called Wormwood. In letter IX the topic of pleasure is addressed. The diabolical principle articulated is the following: "All we can do to encourage the humans to take pleasures which our Enemy (God) has produced, at times, or in ways, or in degrees, which He has forbidden." (cf. *The Screwtape Letters*, New York: The Macmillan Company, 1941, p. 49).

God has invented pleasures, large and small. Their intrinsic goodness is confirmed in the very first chapter of the very first book of the Bible. Yet this goodness has not always been appreciated. Whole philosophies have developed castigating the body and its pleasures. Such is not the philosophy nor the theology of Christianity. Pleasure, in all its appropriate forms, is a means that leads to union and delight.

Realism demands that we face the fact that pleasures are easily and frequently misused. Whether from excess or deprivation, whether through inappropriate circumstances or misguided timing, pleasures can be transformed from life-giving experiences to deadly encounters. The mystery of pleasure demands the manner of grace.

So ingenious is the human spirit, however, that even events that are, in fact, distasteful and deleterious can be perceived or interpreted as though they were life-giving experiences. So clever are we that a *woe*, meant to shake us into reality and lead us into compassion, suddenly becomes, by convulted logic, a *blessing*. A diabolical shrewdness engineers this whole business. Less and less of reality is embraced because of false little feasts of pleasure.

Pleasure and pain, our two constant companions, are central instruments that can lead to union or separation.

* * *

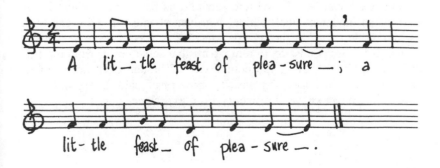

COMMENTARY

Each of us carries around inside an enterprising self that tends to one's own needs, more exactly, wants. The individualistic proverb reminds us that we are to take care of number one and, obviously, that *numero uno* is our own ego. The difficulty here is that we are in the land of half-truth. We must provide for ourselves both out of duty and self-respect. What is missing is that this tending can become a way of life to such a degree that the ego becomes the center of consciousness and there is no interior room nor external action that focuses on God's will or our neighbor's well-being.

Gradually the shrewd old self slips into trickeries and subterfuges so that every whim, wish and want vie to become the driving force of our lives. Unfortunately this process can be so subtle that we are not even aware of what is and has been happening in our hearts for decades. One morning we awake to realize that the home of self is occupied by an enterprising shrew that claims total dominion over our time and energy.

Then, through the action of grace, another self, the "I" that strives to live in the image of God, asserts its presence. Carefully it follows around the old, shrewd, enterprising self, attempting to snatch away the unlawful treasures stolen from life's warehouse. No easy assignment here. Techniques of ingenuity and total self-command outwit the authentic self. This reaches its apex when all is stripped away from the sinful self and, in the midst of this loss and woe, that enterprising being turns the deprivation into a little feast of humility. There is no end to our trickeries.

Can it be that even humility, a foundational virtue that bonds us to a truthful God, can be misused and separate us from our destiny? Is the old self so ingenious that nothing, not even shame and guilt, can push us into the territory of sincere repentance? Can it be that the thievery of love will fail in its mission to remove all that separates us from the true and living God? Such is the complexity of human existence with its valid and invalid feasts of pleasure, showers of pain. Every old man, every old woman knows this history from experience.

Endnotes

All scriptural passages taken from *The New American Bible*, copyright 1970 by the Confraternity of Christian Doctrine, Washington, D.C.

1. *Selected Poetry of Jessica Powers*, edited by Regina Siegfried and Robert F. Morneau (Kansas City, MO.: Sheed & Ward, 1989), p. 37.

2. C.S. Lewis, *The Lion, the Witch and the Wardrobe* (New York: Macmillan Publishing Company, 1950), pp. 114, 118, 120.

3. *Selected Poetry of Jessica Powers*, p. 20.

4. *John Cassian: Conferences*, trans. and preface by Colm Luibheid with introduction by Owen Chadwick (New York: Paulist Press, 1985), pp. 208.

5. *Selected Poetry of Jessica Powers*, p. 23.

6. Johannes Baptist Metz, *Poverty of Spirit*, translated by John Drury (New York: Paulist Press, 1968), p. 53.

7. *Selected Poetry of Jessica Powers*, p. 36.

8. Epistles of St. Paul, cf. *The New American Bible*.

9. *Selected Poetry of Jessica Powers*, p. 65.

10. *The Hidden Ground of Love: The Letters of Thomas Merton on Religious Experience and Social Concerns*, selected and edited by William H. Shannon (New York: Farrar, Straus, Giroux, 1985).

11. *Selected Poetry of Jessica Powers*, p. 48.

12. Hans Urs von Balthasar, *Prayer*, trans. by A. V. Littledale (New York: Sheed & Ward, 1961).

13. *Selected Poetry of Jessica Powers*, p. 150.

118 *Endnotes*

14. Douglas Steere, *On Beginning from Within—On Listening to Another,* (New York: Harper & Row, Publishers, 1943).

15. *Selected Poetry of Jessica Powers,* p. 86.

16. *Letters of Rainer Maria Rilke: 1892-1910,* translated by Jane Bannard Greene and M. D. Herter Norton (New York: W. W. Norton & Company, 1945), pp. 110-112.

17. *Selected Poetry of Jessica Powers,* p. 70.

18. Shannon, *The Hidden Ground of Love,* p. 669.

19. *Selected Poetry of Jessica Powers,* p. 38.

20. *The Simone Weil Reader,* edited by George A. Panichas (New York: David McKay Company, Inc., 1977).

21. *Selected Poetry of Jessica Powers,* p. 81.

22. Henry David Thoreau, *Walden, or Life in the Woods,* with an afterword by Perry Miller (New York: New American Library, 1960).

23. *Selected Poetry of Jessica Powers,* p. 53.

24. *Bernard of Clairvaux: Selected Works,* translation and foreword by G. R. Evans, introduction by Jean Leclercq, O.S.B., preface by Ewert H. Cousins (New York: Paulist Press, 1987).

25. *Selected Poetry of Jessica Powers,* p. 19.

26. Walter Brueggemann, *The Creative Word: Canon as a Model for Biblical Education* (Philadelphia: Fortress Press, 1982).

27. *Selected Poetry of Jessica Powers,* p. 68.

28. Jean-Pierre de Caussade, *The Sacrament of the Present Moment,* translated by Kitty Muggeridge (New York: Harper & Row, Publishers, 1982).

29. *Selected Poetry of Jessica Powers,* p. 117.

30. Madeleine L'Engle, *Walking on Water* (Wheaton, IL.: Harold Shaw Publishers, 1980).